How to do Maths Investigations

by

A. Jamieson, B.Sc.,
Robert Gordon's College, Aberdeen.

ISBN 0 7169 3186 9

© A. Jamieson, 1993.

ROBERT GIBSON · Publisher
17 Fitzroy Place, Glasgow, G3 7SF.

"A mathematician, like an artist or a composer of music, is a creator of patterns."

PREFACE

The subject of Mathematics is now taught and tested under three headings:

 (i) Knowledge and Understanding;
 (ii) Reasoning and Applications;
(iii) Practical Investigations.

It is the third of these elements which presents most difficulty.

Problem Solving in the form of Mathematical Practical Investigations can cause no little anxiety.

The skill of solving such Mathematical Problems can be taught and study of the strategies outlined in this book will help develop the necessary skill and, at the same time, promote the student's confidence.

The book is aimed primarily at students studying for the Scottish Certificate of Education (SCE) Standard Grade Examinations at General or Credit level, but the strategies illustrated will be equally valuable to candidates of the SCE Higher Grade, the SCOTVEC Mathematical Modules or GCSE courses in England and Wales.

In working through this book, the student is advised to attempt each investigation before reading the author's solution. Good solutions to a problem can often be obtained by different means and it is a mistake to think that there is only one correct solution to any problem. Indeed, within the classroom situation, students should be actively encouraged to seek alternative correct solutions to the ones illustrated in the text.

Mathematical Problem Solving is a basic skill which students should retain throughout their lives and apply to problems of the real world, creating and testing conjectures.

CONTENTS

Preface 3
1. Introducing Investigations 5
2. Calculating the Sum of a Series to n Terms 8
3. Finding the nth Term of a Sequence 24
4. Problem-solving with Pythagoras 34
5. Investigating League Fixtures 43
6. Investigating with Circles 49
7. Solving Problems with Simultaneous Equations 77
8. How to Find All the Solutions to a Problem 86
9. Pascal's Triangle 94
10. Exercises Including Some Investigations to try Yourself 98
11. Solutions to Exercises 107

COPYING PROHIBITED

Note: This publication is NOT licensed for copying under the Copyright Licensing Agency's Scheme, to which Robert Gibson & Sons are not party.

All rights reserved. No part of this publication may be reproduced; stored in a retrieval system; or transmitted in any form or by any means — electronic, mechanical, photocopying, or otherwise — without prior permission of the publisher Robert Gibson & Sons, Ltd., 17 Fitzroy Place, Glasgow, G3 7SF.

1. Introducing Investigations

As stated in the Preface, the student is well advised to attempt *any* Investigation on his own before seeking help and before studying a solution offered.

In this book, therefore, an investigation or a number of investigations will be found at the outset in each section, without solutions, and the student should work on these before being tempted to look at solutions set out later in the volume.

The reader should try to write a detailed solution, almost in the form of an essay, and not simply an answer such as a number which he thinks might be the solution. In other words, all answers should be justified.

To set the scene, a sample solution is provided for the first problem.

Problem: Find the last digit in the number 3^{500}.

The initial reaction of every student presented with this problem is to reach for a calculator. This number is too large for most desktop calculators but even if the calculator was programmed to cope with a number of this magnitude, the screen could not be made large enough to take in most of the numbers, far less the last digit, when the number is written out in full.

A calculator may give the value of 3^{20} as 3 486 784 401 but 3^{30} will be given in scientific notation as $2 \cdot 058\ 911\ 321 \times 10^{14}$. This does not mean that the last digit of 3^{30} will be 0 or 1. The number is too large to print on the screen.

How then may we determine the last digit of the number 3^{500}?

Try working out the answer without the aid of a machine. Perhaps you will make some observations which will produce a solution more quickly than you had thought possible.

$3^1 = 3$
$3^2 = 9$
$3^3 = 27$
$3^4 = 81$

$3^5 = 243$
$3^6 = 729$
$3^7 = 2187$
$3^8 = 6561$
$3^9 = 19\,683$
$3^{10} =$ probably ends with the number 9
$3^{11} =$ probably ends with the number 7
$3^{12} =$ probably ends with the number 1

etc.

From these few simple calculations, a pattern has been observed and it should be possible to make a conjecture.

The last digit appears to follow the pattern 3, 9, 7, 1, 3, 9, 7, 1, 3, 9, 7, 1, . . .

Where does the number 3^{500} fit into this pattern?

3^1	3^5	3^9	3^{13}	. . .	3^{497}
3^2	3^6	3^{10}	3^{14}	. . .	3^{498}
3^3	3^7	3^{11}	3^{15}	. . .	3^{499}
3^4	3^8	3^{12}	3^{16}	. . .	3^{500}

Our number 3^{500} would follow the pattern to appear in the fourth row of the 125th column. Just as $3^4, 3^8, 3^{12}, 3^{16}, \ldots$, the number 3^{500} will have as its last digit the number 1.

This simple but systematic approach to the above problem highlights just three of the key strategies to be adopted in our approach to problem-solving, namely:

(a) try simpler cases of the same problem first,
(b) present your findings systematically, perhaps in the form of a table,
(c) look for a pattern to emerge from these simpler cases.

One aim of this book is to outline how to use these and other tactics.

It is advised that the following strategies should be considered when you are faced with problems of an investigative nature.

1. Read and try to understand what is being asked. If you are not sure what is being asked after two or three readings, then ask to have the question explained to you. (It is better to ask than to spend the whole of the allotted time writing an irrelevant dissertation.)

2. Draw a diagram if at all possible.
3. Try to think of an analogous problem which you may have solved, perhaps from this book.
4. If the problem appears to be too difficult to attempt directly, then it is very possible, like many of the investigations in this book, that you are expected to consider similar but simpler problems first.
5. By presenting your findings in the form of a table, try to establish a pattern from these simpler cases.
6. Try to generalise your results, i.e. find a formula for the nth term of the pattern.
7. Examine your solution, i.e. check your conjecture, ensuring that your formula is correct.

These strategies are listed here in the *Introduction* for easy reference.

Try this problem yourself.

[Find the last digit of the number 2^{90}

Answer: 4]

2. Calculating the Sum of a Series to n Terms

As many investigations involve the addition of the first n natural numbers, we shall devote the first few paragraphs of this unit to this concept.

Question:

Find the sum of the following:
$$1 + 2 + 3 + 4 + 5 + 6 + 7 + 8 + 9 + 10$$

Solution:

Rather than simply adding these ten numbers together, here is an unorthodox but interesting way to carry out the calculation.

sum = $1 + 2 + 3 + 4 + 5 + 6 + 7 + 8 + 9 + 10$ —— ①
also sum = $10 + 9 + 8 + 7 + 6 + 5 + 4 + 3 + 2 + 1$ —— ②
Adding ① and ② gives
  twice sum = $11 + 11 + 11 + 11 + 11 + 11 + 11 + 11 + 11 + 11$
i.e. twice sum = 11×10
       = 110
hence sum = $\dfrac{110}{2}$
       = 55

Now why should we want to add our ten numbers in this unorthodox way? The reason becomes clear if we consider the following question which would involve a laborious calculation if we were to add the numbers together one after the other.

Question:

Calculate $1 + 2 + 3 + 4 + 5 + \ldots + 100$

Solution:

sum = $1 + 2 + 3 + 4 + 5 + \ldots + 100$ ——— ①
sum = $100 + 99 + 98 + 97 + 96 + \ldots + 1$ ——— ②
Adding ① and ② gives
  twice sum = $101 + 101 + 101 + 101 + 101 + \ldots + 101$
i.e. twice sum = 101×100
hence sum = $\dfrac{10100}{2} = 5050$

Of course, this method may be used to calculate the sum of this series to as many terms as we wish.

Now to find the sum of the series to *n* terms.

Question:

Calculate $1 + 2 + 3 + 4 + 5 + \ldots + n$

Solution:

$$\text{sum} = 1 + \quad 2 + \quad 3 + 4 + 5 + \ldots + (n-2) + (n-1) + n \quad —①$$
$$\text{sum} = n + (n-1) + (n-2) + \ldots\ldots + 5 + 4 + 3 + \quad 2 + 1 \quad —②$$

Adding ① and ② produces

$$\text{twice sum} = (n+1) + (n+1) + (n+1) + (n+1) + \ldots + (n+1)$$
$$= n(n+1)$$

hence $\quad \text{sum} = \frac{1}{2}n(n+1)$

Although it is in the student's interest to memorise this formula, it is equally important to be able to justify it as illustrated above.

> The sum to **n** terms of the series $1 + 2 + 3 + 4 + 5 + \ldots + n$
> is found by $\frac{1}{2}n(n+1)$

Investigation 1: *Staircase*

The staircase shown opposite is 5 stairs high. How many cubes are required to build this staircase?
(Show all your working.)

How many cubes would be required to build a similar staircase but 365 stairs high?

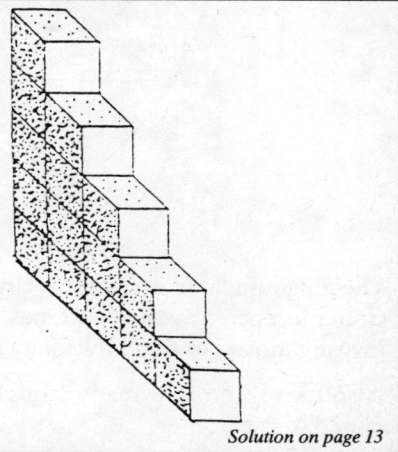

Solution on page 13

Investigation 2: *Counting Rectangles*

How many rectangles of any size are contained in the above diagram?

Solution on page 13

Investigation 3: *Chord Counting*

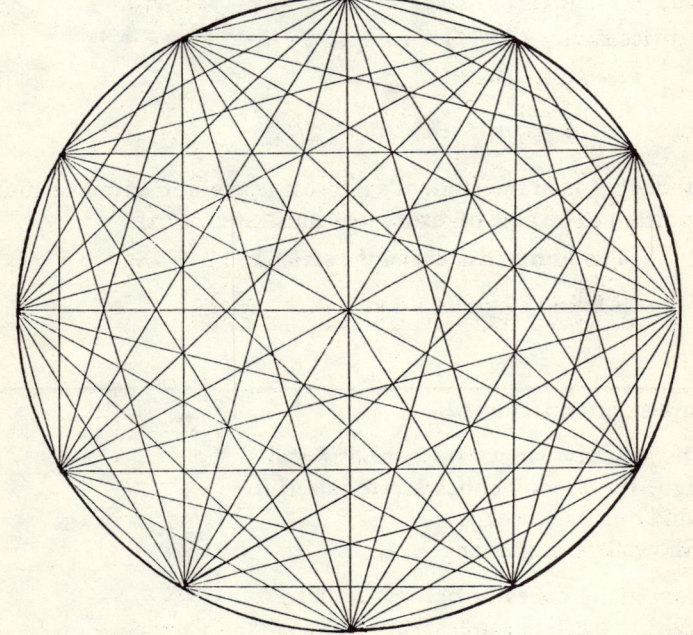

The diagram above shows a circle which has 12 points marked on the circumference. Every point has been joined to every other point. The investigation is to find how many straight lines (chords) are in the diagram.

Also try to find how many straight lines are in a circle which has n points joined to each other.

Solution on page 15

Investigation 4: *The Chessboard Problem*

Question:

How many squares are there in a chessboard? (Not 64!)

Solution on page 18

Investigation 5: *Odeon of Herodes Atticus*

At the Acropolis in Athens there is a restored outdoor theatre in which every year a festival of music and drama is held — the Odeon of Herodes Atticus.

The seating plan of the Odeon is in the form of a sector of a circle.

There is space in the front step for twelve people to sit comfortably and each step has accommodation for eight more people than the one in front of it.

(a) Find the capacity of the theatre, given that there are thirty-three steps to house the audience.

(b) Find the capacity of **any** similarly designed theatre. *Solution on page 21*

Before we look at a solution to the problem, first let us go over again the seven strategies outlined in Section 1 — Introducing Investigations.

1. Ensure that you know what is being asked.
2. Draw a diagram.
3. Try to relate to an analogous problem.
4. Consider similar but simpler cases of the same problem.
5. Present findings in a table to help establish a pattern.
6. Generalise your results, i.e. find a formula for the nth term within the pattern.
7. Check your conjecture.

Solution to Investigation 1: *Staircase*

To build the staircase 5 stairs high, we require $1 + 2 + 3 + 4 + 5$ cubes, i.e. 15 cubes.

To build a staircase 365 stairs high we would require $1 + 2 + 3 + 4 + 5 + \ldots + 365$ cubes.

$$\text{sum} = 1 + 2 + 3 + 4 + 5 + \ldots + 365 \quad\text{①}$$
$$\text{sum} = 365 + 364 + 363 + \ldots\ldots\ldots + 1 \quad\text{②}$$

Adding ① and ② gives

twice sum $= 366 + 366 + 366 + 366 + \ldots + 366$

twice sum $= 366 \times 365$

$$\text{sum} = \frac{1}{2}(366)(365) = 183 \times 365 = 66\,795$$

Solution to Investigation 2: *Counting Rectangles*

Clearly we cannot hope to count all the rectangles enclosed in the figure. Our approach, as in many investigations, should be to consider a similar but simpler problem first.

Let us consider the figure

There is obviously 1 rectangle.

Now consider the figure

There are 3 rectangles, i.e.

Now consider this figure

it contains 6 rectangles

The next figure in the pattern contains 10 rectangles.
(Draw the rectangles to prove this!)

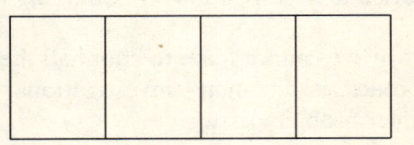

The results obtained from the simpler problems can now be tabulated.

Figure	1	2	3	4	5	6	7	20	n
Number of Rectangles	1	3	6	10	15	21	28		

                              +2   +3   +4   +5   +6   +7

By presenting the results in a table we may be able to see a pattern as shown. If we continue the pattern it will be possible to solve the original problem.

The original figure is the 7th in the sequence which proves to contain 28 rectangles.

This answer is the sum $1 + 2 + 3 + 4 + 5 + 6 + 7 = 28$

The investigation should not be terminated here.

What about the nth figure of the sequence?

The number of rectangles contained within the nth figure is calculated by

$$1 + 2 + 3 + 4 + 5 + \ldots + n$$

the sum of which was shown earlier to be $\frac{1}{2}n(n + 1)$.

Hence the number of rectangles contained within the 20th figure is

$\frac{1}{2}(20)(20 + 1) = \frac{1}{2}(20)(21) = 210$.

Now complete the table on page 14 by adding in the last two results.

Solution to Investigation 3:   *Chord Counting*

Try simpler cases first, i.e. a circle with only two points on the circumference, then a circle with three points, then four and five.

Two points —
one line

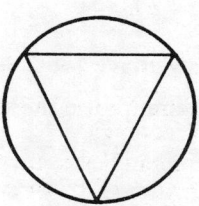

Three points —
three lines

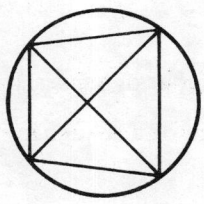

Four points —
six lines

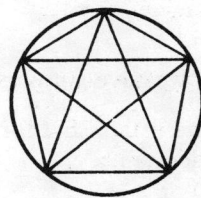

Five points —
ten lines

By presenting these findings in a table, we may recognise a pattern to help us solve the original problem.

Number of points	1	2	3	4	5	6	12	n
Number of lines	0	1	3	6	10	15		

   +1 +2 +3 +4 +5

Again the numbers which appear in the table are found by adding 1, then 2, then 3, etc.

For 2 points we have 1 line.
For 3 points we have $1 + 2$ lines.
For 4 points we have $1 + 2 + 3$ lines.
For 5 points we have $1 + 2 + 3 + 4$ lines.
.
.
.
For 12 points we have $1 + 2 + 3 + 4 + 5 + 6 + 7 + 8 + 9 + 10 + 11$ lines
$= 66$ lines
.
.
.

For n points we have $1 + 2 + 3 + 4 + 5 + \ldots + (n-1)$ lines.
To find this sum we use the same method as before.

$$\text{sum} = \quad 1 + \quad 2 + \quad 3 + 4 + 5 + \ldots + (n-1) \quad —\!—\!— \text{①}$$
$$\text{sum} = (n-1) + (n-2) + (n-3) + \ldots\ldots\ldots + \quad 1 \quad —\!—\!— \text{②}$$

Adding ① and ② gives
 twice sum $= n + n + n + n + n + n + \ldots + n$
This time there are $(n-1)$ terms and so
 twice sum $= n(n-1)$
hence sum $= \frac{1}{2}n(n-1)$

Therefore if we have n points on our circle the number of lines is $\frac{1}{2}n(n-1)$.

Whenever we establish a formula for the nth term of a sequence, we should test our conjecture.

If nth term $= \frac{1}{2}n(n-1)$ then

12th term $= \frac{1}{2} \times 12 \times 11 = 66$ lines which is correct from above and so this answer, together with our general formula, can be added to our table above.

In each of the previous investigations the sequence of numbers, 1, 3, 6, 10, 15, 21, . . . has appeared. These numbers are known as the triangular numbers. The figures below illustrate why they are known as the triangular numbers.

The figures below help us identify the square numbers

i.e. 1, 4, 9, 16, 25, 36, . . .

Solution to Investigation 4: The Chessboard Problem

Again we could not hope to count all the squares of various sizes contained within the chessboard.

As before we consider similar but simpler situations.

Consider a 1 × 1 grid — there is 1 square

we investigate a 2 × 2 grid — there are 1 + 4 squares i.e. 5 squares

with a 3 × 3 grid — there are 1 + 4 + 9 squares

Within a 4 × 4 grid — we have 1 + 4 + 9 + 16 squares

i.e. we have 1

we have 4

we have 9

and we have 16

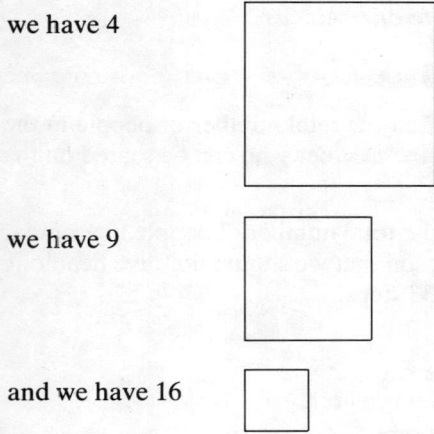

To return to our original problem of the chessboard which is an 8 × 8 grid, it follows that the total number of squares contained within the board is 1 + 4 + 9 + 16 + 25 + 36 + 49 + 64, i.e. the sum of the first 8 square numbers = 204.

Now we should try to generalise our result by considering the number of squares within an $n \times n$ grid.

Since the numbers of squares within an 8 × 8 grid is found by

$$1^2 + 2^2 + 3^2 + 4^2 + 5^2 + 6^2 + 7^2 + 8^2$$

then the number of squares with an $n \times n$ grid will be

$$1^2 + 2^2 + 3^2 + 4^2 + 5^2 + \ldots + n^2$$

Although it is beyond the scope of this discussion to prove the formula below, the student may like to verify that *the sum of the first n square numbers* can be found by

$$\frac{1}{6}n(n + 1)(2n + 1)$$

Now that we have learned how to carry out the arithmetic involved in finding the sum of the first n natural numbers, let us now consider an investigation which illustrates the strategies outlined in the Introduction to this text.

Solution to Investigation 5: *Odeon of Herodes Atticus*

1. **Ensure that you know exactly what is asked.**

   In this problem we are required to find the **total** number of people in the theatre when it is filled and not just the number who can be seated on the 33rd step.

   We also need to find a formula for the total number of people in a similar theatre with *n* steps. It is for this reason that we should not dive headlong into the problem and consider only 33 steps.

2. **Draw a diagram.**

   The diagram below makes the problem clearer.

   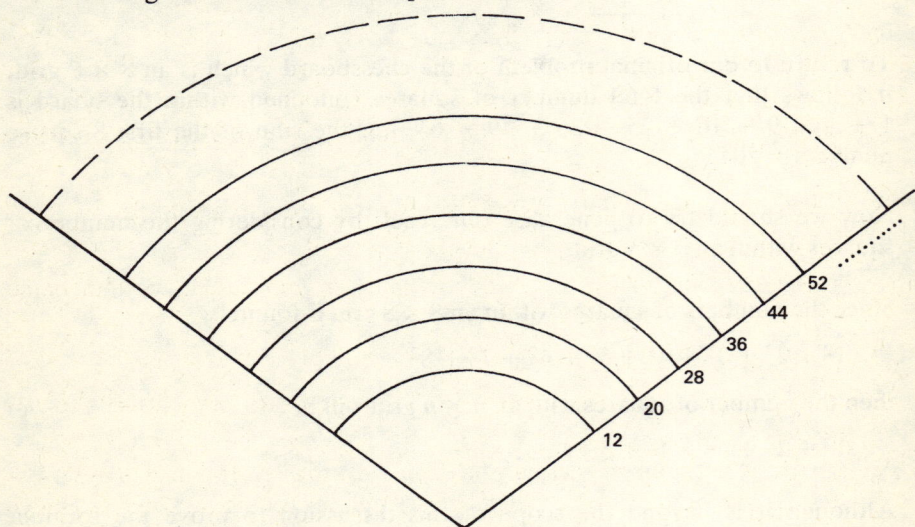

3. **Think of an analogous problem.**

   Clearly we have to find the sum of a series. Although the numbers in the series are not simply consecutive natural numbers as in previous illustrations in this chapter, we should be able to adopt the method used earlier.

4. **Consider similar but simpler cases of the same problem.**

   Let us first consider 1, 2, 3, 4, 5, etc., steps before going for 33 steps.

5. **Present findings in a table to help establish a pattern.**

Step Number	Number of People
1	12
2	12 + 8
3	12 + 8 + 8 or 12 + 2 × 8
4	12 + 8 + 8 + 8 or 12 + 3 × 8
5	12 + 8 + 8 + 8 + 8 or 12 + 4 × 8

Already a pattern is apparent from the table. The number seated on the 6th step must be 12 + 5 × 8 and the number on the 33rd step would be 12 + 32 × 8.

6. **Generalise your results, i.e. find the nth term within the pattern.**

It follows that the number on the nth step would be $12 + (n-1) \times 8$.

This expression, which represents the number who can be accommodated on the nth step, may be simplified to $12 + 8n - 8$ or $8n + 4$.

7. **Check your conjecture.**

It is proposed that the number who can be seated on the nth row is $8n + 4$.

Check: The number who can be seated on the 6th row is $8 \times 6 + 4 = 48 + 4 = 52$, which is correct according to our sequence 12, 20, 28, 36, 44, 52, . . .

Of course, we have not yet anwered the investigation but have merely found a formula for the number accommodated on each row.

To find the total number in the filled theatre with 33 rows, we must find the sum of the series

12 + 20 + 28 + 36 + 44 + 52 + . . . to 33 terms.

Also, to find the total number in a similar theatre with n rows, we must find the sum of the series

12 + 20 + 28 + 36 + 44 + 52 + . . . to n terms.

How do we approach this?

Think of an analogous problem.

We can use the same technique as was illustrated earlier in the chapter.

The 33rd term is $12 + 32 \times 8 = 12 + 256 = 268$.

sum = $12 + 20 + 28 + 36 + 44 + 52 + \ldots + 268$ ——— ①

Also, writing the series in reverse,

sum = $268 + 260 + 252 + 244 + 236 + 228 + \ldots + 12$ ——— ②

Adding ① and ② gives

twice sum = $280 + 280 + 280 + 280 + 280 + 280 + \ldots + 280$ to 33 terms.

Hence

twice sum = 280×33

and so

$$\text{sum} = \frac{280 \times 33}{2}$$

$$= 4620$$

Conclusion:

The capacity of the Odeon of Herodes Atticus is 4620.

Now we shall generalise the result by carrying out a similar calculation for a similarly designed theatre with n rows.

The nth term is $12 + (n-1) \times 8 = 12 + 8n - 8 = 8n + 4$.

sum = $12 + 20 + 28 + 36 + 44 + 52 + \ldots + (8n + 4)$ ——— ①

Also, writing the series in reverse,

sum = $(8n + 4) + (8n - 4) + (8n - 12) + (8n - 20) + (8n - 28) + \ldots + 12$ ——— ②

Adding ① and ② gives

twice sum = $(8n + 16) + (8n + 16) + (8n + 16) + (8n + 16) + (8n + 16) + (8n + 16) + \ldots + (8n + 16)$ to n terms.

Hence,
twice sum $= (8n + 16) \times n$
and so

$$\begin{aligned} \text{sum} &= \frac{1}{2}(8n + 16) \times n \\ &= (4n + 8) \times n \\ &= 4n^2 + 8n \\ &= 4n(n + 2). \end{aligned}$$

This expression represents the total number of people who can be accommodated in a theatre of a similar design to the Odeon of Herodes Atticus but with n steps.

Check your conjecture.

It is proposed that the number who can be seated with n rows is $4n(n + 2)$.

Check: The number who can be seated in the first 6 rows is $(4 \times 6)(6 + 8)$
$$= 24 \times 8$$
$$= 192$$
which is correct according to our series $12 + 20 + 28 + 36 + 44 + 52 = 192$.

Conclusion:

The capacity of the Odeon of Herodes Atticus is 4620.

The capacity of any similarly designed theatre having n rows of seats is $4n(n + 2)$.

Strategies Summarised.

List of strategies to be followed.
1. Read and try to understand what is being asked.
2. Draw a diagram if at all possible.
3. Try to think of an analogous problem which you may have solved.
4. If the problem appears to be too difficult to attempt directly, then consider similar but simpler cases first.
5. By presenting your findings in the form of a table, try to establish a pattern from these simpler cases.
6. Try to generalise your results, i.e. find a formula for the nth term of the pattern.
7. Examine your solution, i.e. check your conjecture ensuring that your formula is correct.

3. Finding the *n*th term of a sequence

As many practical investigations require the student to spot patterns and to find a general solution to the problem, the following pages are written to help the student methodically find formulae for the *n*th term of various sequences.

Investigation 6: *Toothpicks*

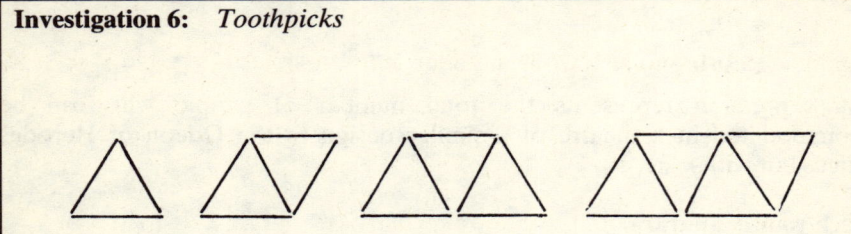

Toothpicks are arranged to form a pattern of triangles as shown above. A box contains 255 toothpicks. Is it possible to continue the above pattern by using the whole contents of the box? If so, how many triangles are formed?

Solution on page 25

Investigation 7: *Hexagons*

Join the dots below to make a pattern of hexagons.

If we continue the pattern below, how many lines need to be drawn to form the 100th figure containing 100 hexagons?

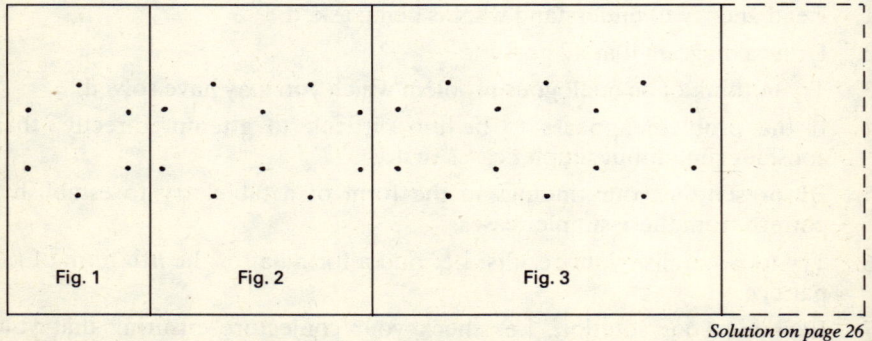

Solution on page 26

Solution to Investigation 6: *Toothpicks*

First we set up a table.

Number of Triangles	1	2	3	4	5	6	n	
Number of Toothpicks	3	5	7	9	11	13		255

First Difference: +2   +2   +2   +2   +2

and now look for a pattern. It appears that there is a difference of +2 between the terms in the bottom row. We shall refer to this as the 'First Difference'.

Now we should look for a formula for the nth term of the sequence, i.e. try to establish the number of toothpicks needed to construct n triangles in the given pattern.

Theorem

Any sequence which has a constant 'First Difference' of 'a' takes the form nth term = $an + b$.

Proof:

Term	1	2	3	4	5
Number	$a+b$	$2a+b$	$3a+b$	$4a+b$	$5a+b$

First Difference: a a a a

In the above table the nth term = $an + b$ where n has been given values 1, 2, 3, 4, 5, ...

Returning to our toothpick problem, since we have a constant 'First Difference' of +2 the nth term of our sequence = $an + b$, where $a = +2$, i.e. nth term = $2n + b$.

Now it is easy to find b by selecting one of the terms, e.g. 3rd term = 7

since nth term = $2n + b$

then 3rd term = $2(3) + b = 7$
              = $6 + b = 7$

and so $b = 1$.

The formula for the nth term of our sequence = $2n + 1$.

We should now test our conjecture by choosing another term, e.g. 5th term.
If nth term $= 2n + 1$ then 5th term $= 2(5) + 1 = 11$ which is correct.

Number of Triangles	1	2	3	4	5	6	n	
Number of Toothpicks	3	5	7	9	11	13	$2n + 1$	255

We are now ready to answer the question: Is it possible to continue the pattern of triangles using 255 toothpicks?

Solve the equation
$$2n + 1 = 255$$
$$2n = 254$$
$$n = 127.$$

As n is a whole number it is possible to use all 255 toothpicks in the given pattern, producing 127 triangles.

Solution to Investigation 7: *Hexagons*

We shall present our observations in the form of a table as usual.

Number of Hexagons	1	2	3	4	5	n	100
Number of Lines	6	11	16	21	26		

First Difference: +5   +5   +5   +5

Again we have a sequence with a constant 'First Difference' — this time +5, indicating that the nth term takes the form $an + b$, where $a = 5$.
nth term $= 5n + b$

Selecting the 3rd term $= 5(3) + b = 16$, i.e. $15 + b = 16$
and so $b = 1$.
nth term $= 5n + 1$ This result may be inserted in the above table.

We can now find the 100th term of the sequence:
100th term $= 5(100) + 1 = 501$

To form 100 hexagons in the given pattern we require to draw 501 lines.

EXERCISES

The student should reinforce the concept stated in the last two investigations by finding the *n*th term of the following sequences and completing the tables below.

(i)
Term	1	2	3	4	5	20	*n*	
Number	7	11	15	19	23			127

(ii)
Term	1	2	3	4	5	50	*n*	
Number	2	8	14	20	26			596

(iii)
Term	1	2	3	4	5	10	*n*	
Number	9	18	27	36				630

(iv)
Term	1	2	3	4	5	6	*n*	
Number	2	5		11		17		50

(v)
Term	1	2	3	4	5	6	*n*	
Number	$1\frac{1}{2}$	2	$2\frac{1}{2}$	3	$3\frac{1}{2}$	4		61

(vi) Draw the next diagram in the sequence of patterns below and complete the table.

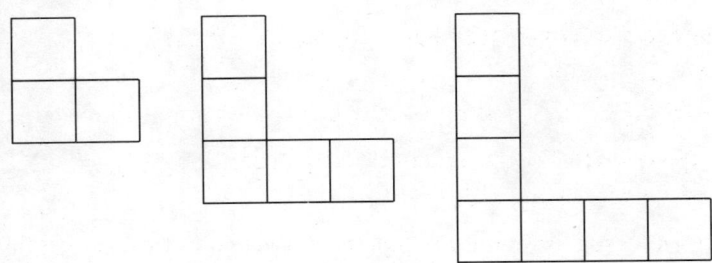

Pattern	1	2	3	4	5	*n*	100
Number of Squares			9				

Answers on next page.

ANSWERS

(i) 83, $4n + 3$, 31

(ii) 296, $6n - 4$, 100

(iii) 45, 90, $9n$, 70

(iv) 8, 14, $3n - 1$, 17

(v) $\frac{1}{2}n + 1$, 120

(vi) 3, 5, 7, 11, $2n + 1$, 201

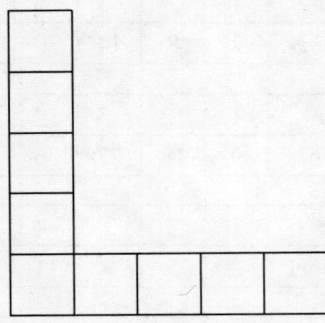

Investigation 8: *Grids*

In this 1st diagram there are 4 connecting pipes in the grid.

In this 2nd diagram there are 12 connecting pipes in the grid.

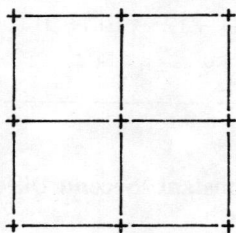

In this 3rd diagram the student should count the number of connecting pipes by drawing them in, following the pattern of the diagrams above.

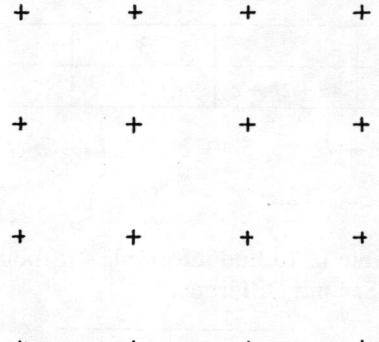

By completing the following table, find the number of connecting pipes in the 25th diagram of the sequence.

Diagram Number	1	2	3	4	5	n	25
Number of Pipes	4	12	24	40	60		

Solution on page 30

Solution to Investigation 8: *Grids*

As we did previously, we look for the *n*th term of the sequence. First we investigate the 'First Difference' between the terms. It is obvious that this time there is no constant 'First Difference', which indicates that the *n*th term does not take the form $an + b$.

We will now investigate the 'Second Difference' ...

Diagram Number	1	2	3	4	5	n	25
Number of Pipes	4	12	24	40	60		

First Difference   +8 +12 +16 +20
Second Difference   +4   +4   +4

Theorem:

Any sequence which has a constant 'Second Difference' of $2a$ takes the form *n*th term $= an^2 + bn + c$

In the table below, the *n*th term $= an^2 + bn + c$ where *n* has been given values 1, 2, 3, 4, 5, ...

Proof:

Term	1	2	3	4	5
Number	$a+b+c$	$4a+2b+c$	$9a+3b+c$	$16a+4b+c$	$25a+5b+c$

First Difference $3a+b$ $5a+b$ $7a+b$ $9a+b$ (not constant)
Second Difference: $2a$ $2a$ $2a$

This theorem will enable us to find a formula for the *n*th term of a sequence which has a constant 'Second Difference'.

Returning to the *grid* problem which results in a sequence with a constant 'Second Difference' of +4.
The *n*th term $= an^2 + bn + c$ where $2a = 4$, i.e. $a = 2$
The *n*th term $= 2n^2 + bn + c$

To enable us to find the values of *b* and *c*, we select any two terms from our table above, e.g. 1st term = 4   and   2nd term = 12.

As the nth term $= 2n^2 + bn + c$
1st term $= 2(1)^2 + b(1) + c = 4$ ——— ①
2nd term $= 2(2)^2 + b(2) + c = 12$ ——— ②
1st term $= 2 + b + c = 4$ ——— ①
2nd term $= 8 + 2b + c = 12$ ——— ②
Hence $\quad\quad\quad b + c = 2$ ——— ①
and $\quad\quad\quad 2b + c = 4$ ——— ②

If we now subtract equation ① from equation ② we obtain $b = 2$.

To find c we substitute the value for b into equation ① above.

Hence $2 + c = 2$, giving $c = 0$.

With $a = 2$, $b = 2$, $c = 0$, we are now able to state the formula for the nth term of the sequence:

$\quad\quad n$th term $= an^2 + bn + c$ becomes $2n^2 + 2n \quad$ or $\quad 2n(n + 1)$.

Now to test our conjecture by selecting one of the known terms:
3rd term $= 2(3)^2 + 2(3) = 19 + 6 = 24 \quad$ which is correct.

We can now add this formula to the given table and use it to answer the original question which was:

How many pipes would be drawn in the 25th diagram in the sequence of grids?

25th term $= 2(25)^2 + 2(25)$
$\quad\quad\quad\quad = 2(625) + 50$
$\quad\quad\quad\quad = 1250 + 50$
$\quad\quad\quad\quad = 1300$

Answer: $\quad$ 1300 pipes.

EXERCISES

The student should reinforce the idea of the last investigation by finding the nth term of the following sequences and completing the tables below.

(i)

Term	1	2	3	4	5	6	n
Number	2	6	12	20	30		

(ii)

Term	1	2	3	4	5	6	n
Number	0	9	22	39	60	85	

(iii)

Term	1	2	3	4	5	6	n
Number	1	3	6	10	15	21	

(iv)

Term	1	2	3	4	5	6	n
Number	0	2	6	12	20	30	

(v)

Term	1	2	3	4	5	6	n
Number	11	14	19	26	35		

Answers on next page.

ANSWERS

(i)

Term	1	2	3	4	5	6	n
Number	2	6	12	20	30	42	$n^2 + n$

(ii)

Term	1	2	3	4	5	6	n
Number	0	9	22	39	60	85	$2n^2 + 3n - 5$

(iii)

Term	1	2	3	4	5	6	n
Number	1	3	6	10	15	21	$\frac{1}{2}n^2 + \frac{1}{2}n$

(iv)

Term	1	2	3	4	5	6	n
Number	0	2	6	12	20	30	$n^2 - n$

(v)

Term	1	2	3	4	5	6	n
Number	11	14	19	26	35	46	$n^2 + 10$

4. Problem-Solving with Pythagoras

Pythagoras' Jigsaw

To show that area A = area B + area C in the diagram below copy the figure and follow these instructions:

1. By lightly drawing the diagonals in pencil find the centre of square C.
2. Draw a line parallel to the *hypotenuse* of the triangle passing through the centre of square C.
3. Draw a line perpendicular to the *hypotenuse* of the triangle passing through the centre of square C.
4. The lines drawn on square C will have divided square C into four congruent quadrilaterals, i.e. quadrilaterals of the same size and shape. Label the four pieces 1, 2, 3 and 4.
5. Label square B as piece 5.
6. Carefully cut out pieces 1, 2, 3, 4 and 5.
7. The five pieces should now be placed to fit on top of square A.
8. If the five pieces can be arranged to completely cover square A then you have proved that area A = area B + area C, i.e.

    "The square on the hypotenuse of a right-angled triangle is equal to the sum of the squares on the other two sides."

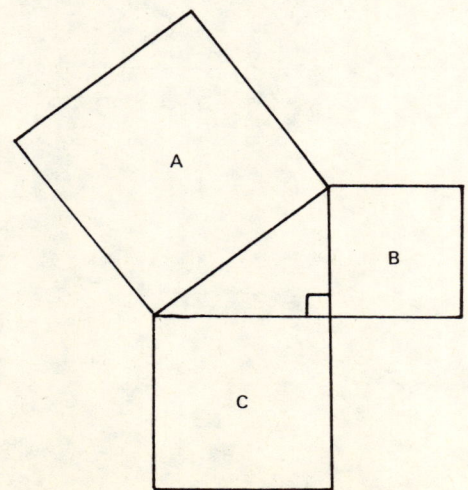

Investigation 9: *Oil Pipes*

The diagram below shows oil pipes stored in such a way that they are safely stacked.

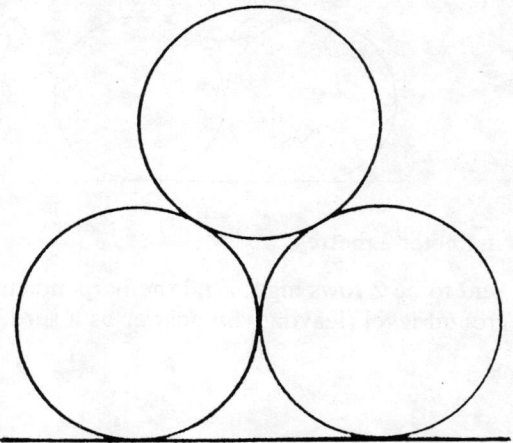

Each oil pipe has diameter 2 metres. Investigate the relationship between the number of rows and the height of the stack.

Solution on page 40

The diagram below shows 3 oil pipes stored in such a way that they are safely stacked.

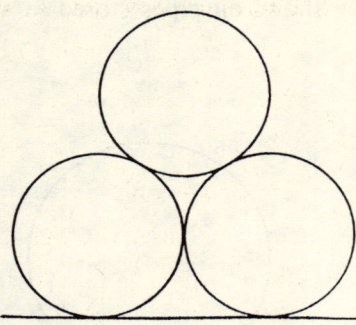

Each oil pipe has diameter 2 metres.

(a) This stack is said to be 2 rows high. Find the perpendicular height of the stack above ground level (leaving you answer as a surd, i.e. in the form $a + \sqrt{b}$).

(b) As an additional safety factor, a triangular casing is placed around the stack as shown below.

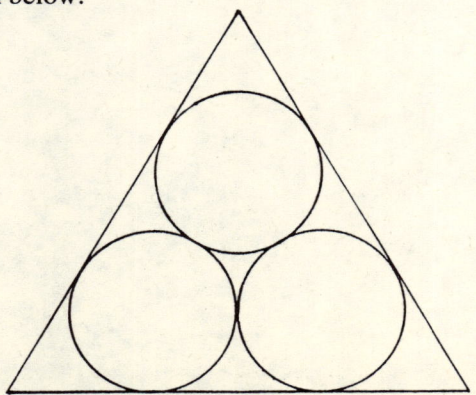

By following the instructions below, make an accurate construction of the previous figure which shows the end view of the stacked pipes in the casing. Use only a pair of compasses and a straight edege.

1. First construct the equilateral triangle PQR.
2. Construct the perpendicular bisectors of the sides of the triangle.
3. Draw these bisectors, naming them QS, RT and PU.
4. Bisect the angle PSQ, naming the bisector SV, where V lies on PU.
5. Using compasses, with radius set to the length of PV, mark QW on the line QS. Similarly mark RX on the line RT.
6. Draw the three required circles with centres V, W and X.

As safety is paramount in the oil industry, employees are told that when storing pipes they must be stacked using this pattern.

(c) This stack is 3 rows high. Find the perpendicular height of this stack above ground level, leaving your answer as a surd (i.e. in the form of $a + c\sqrt{b}$).

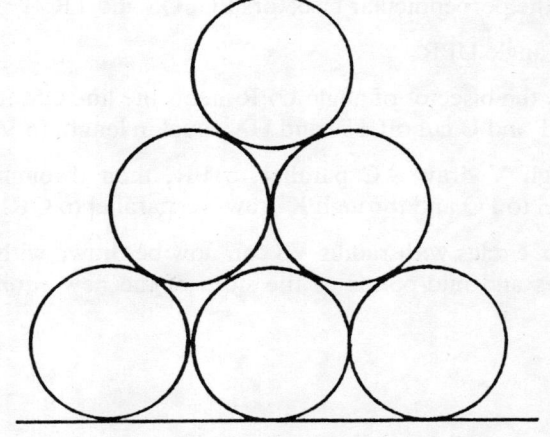

(d) The figure below shows the 3 row stack plus casing. By following these instructions and using only a pair of compasses, a straight edge and a set square make an accurate construction of this figure.

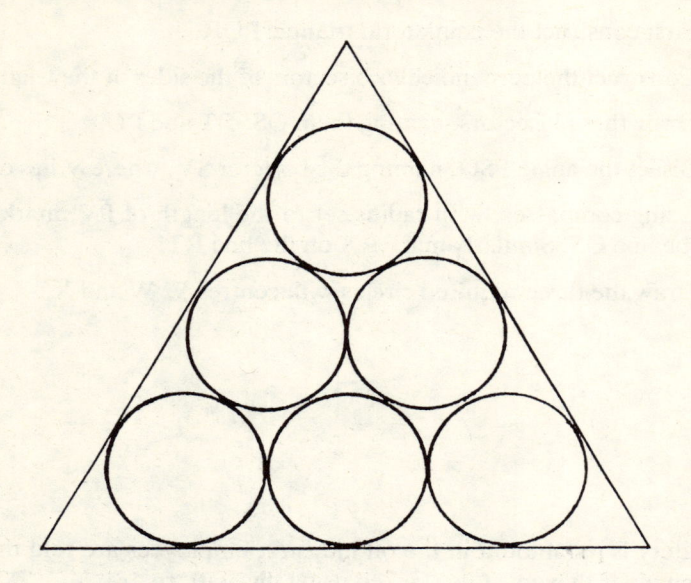

1. Draw equilateral triangle PQR.
2. Bisect each side of the triangle.
3. Draw the perpendicular bisectors PU, QS and TR.
4. Bisect angle UPR.
5. Where the bisector of angle UPR meets the line QS, mark a point V. From T and U cut off TW and UX equal in length to VS.
6. Through V draw AC parallel to PR, then through W draw AB parallel to PQ and through X draw BC parallel to QR.
7. The six circles with radius VS can now be drawn with centres at the vertices and mid-points of the sides of the new equilateral triangle ABC.

(e) Now find the perpendicular height of this 4 row stack above ground level, again leaving your answer in the form $a + c\sqrt{b}$.

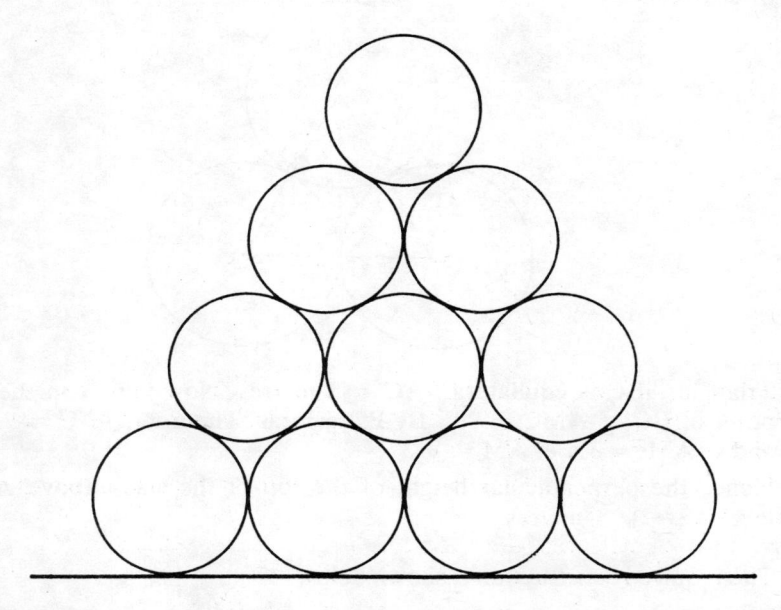

(f) Investigate the relationship between the number of rows and the height of the stack.

(g) For safety reasons the stack should be no more than 20 metres high. Calculate the maximum number of **pipes** which can be stored in one stack.

Students should note that in this Investigation credit would be given for accuracy in the constructions.

Solutions to Investigation 9 — *Oil Pipes:*

(a) To find the perpendicular height, first we should join the centres of the three circles.

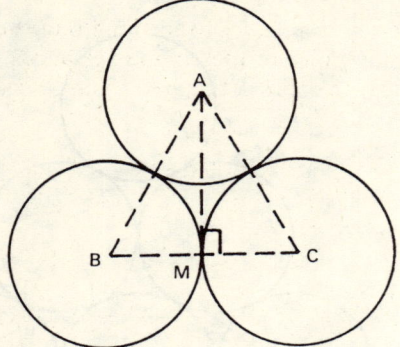

Triangle ABC is equilateral. AC = 2 metres. Now join A to the midpoint of BC. $\angle AMC = 90°$. By Pythagoras' Theorem, $AM^2 = 2^2 - 1^2$ and so $AM^2 = 3$, i.e. $AM = \sqrt{3}$.

Hence the perpendicular height of the top of the stack above ground level is $2 + \sqrt{3}$ metres.

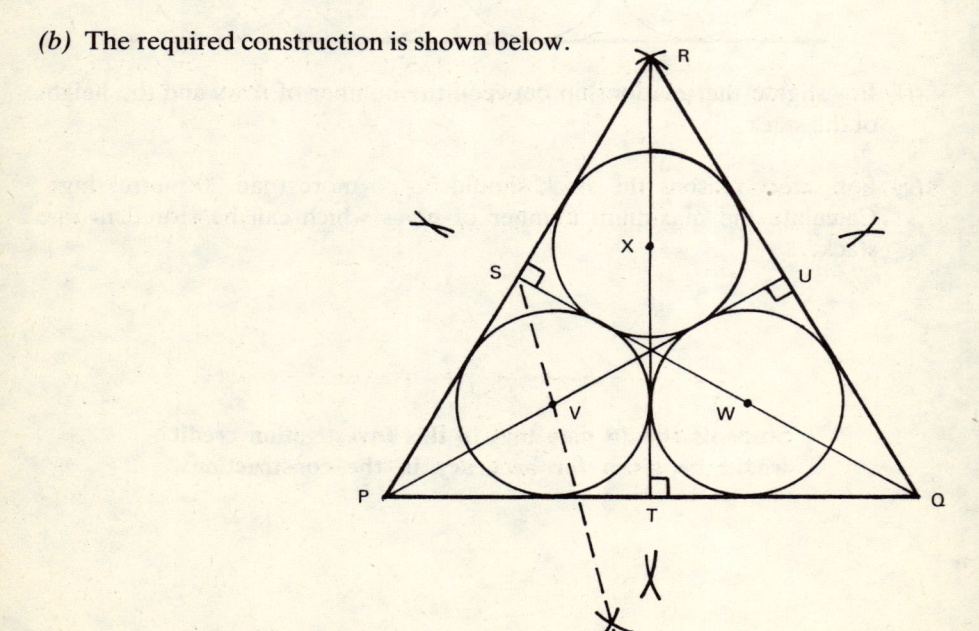

(b) The required construction is shown below.

(c) Using the same method as was illustrated for part (a), the height of the top of a three row stack above ground level is $2 + 2\sqrt{3}$ metres.

(d) The construction for the three row stack is shown below.

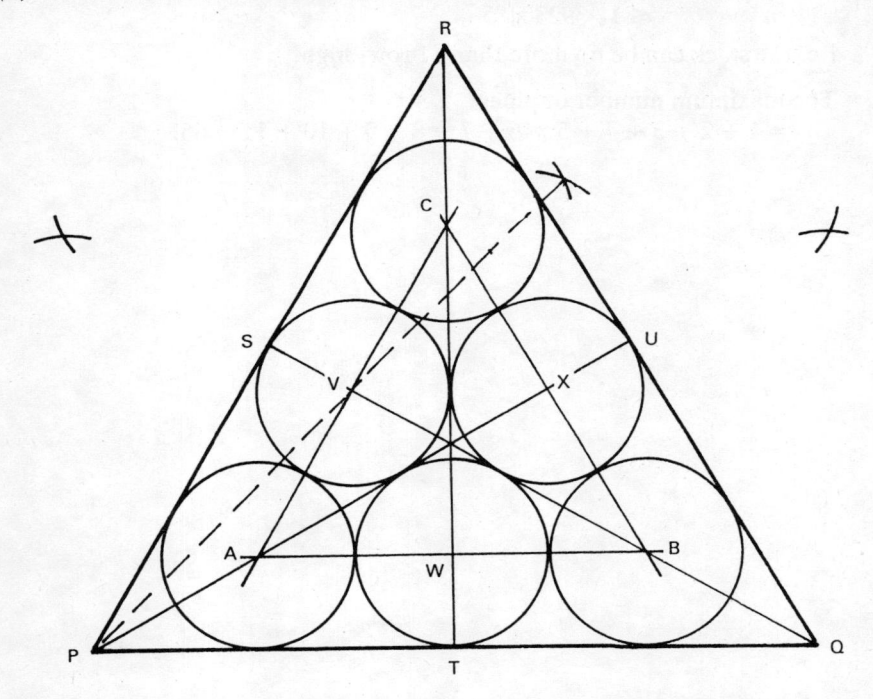

(e) The height of the top of a four row stack above ground level is $2 + 3\sqrt{3}$ metres.

(f) To establish a connection between the number of rows and the height of the stack we construct a table.

Number of rows	1	2	3	4	n
Height of stack (in metres)	2	$2 + \sqrt{3}$	$2 + 2\sqrt{3}$	$2 + 3\sqrt{3}$	$2 + (n-1)\sqrt{3}$

(g) $2 + (n-1)\sqrt{3} \leq 20$
    $(n-1)\sqrt{3} \leq 18$
    $(n-1) \leq 18 \div \sqrt{3}$
    $(n-1) \leq 10 \cdot 39230485\ldots$
    $n \leq 11 \cdot 39230485\ldots$

i.e. the stack can be no more than 11 rows high.

The maximum number of pipes
    $= 1 + 2 + 3 + 4 + 5 + 6 + 7 + 8 + 9 + 10 + 11 = 66.$

5. Investigating League Fixtures

Investigation 10: *Inter-House Competition*

A school organises an inter-house hockey tournament to be decided on a league basis. At the tournament, each of the four houses, Albyn, Blackfriars, Collyhill and Dunnoter, plays against each other house once only.

(i) How many games are played altogether?

(ii) If there were twelve teams in the competition, how many games would have to be played?

(iii) Investigate further.

Solution on page 44

Investigation 11: *Football Leagues*

Teams in football leagues play each other at home and away.

How many games were played in the Scottish Premier League during the season 1990–91? (There were 10 teams in the league during that season.)

Solution on page 45

Investigation 12: *Restructured Football League*

At the beginning of the 1991–92 football season, the Scottish Premier League was restructured whereby the number of teams within the league was changed from ten to twelve.

How many more games had to be played as a result of this change?

Solution on page 48

Solution to Investigation 10: *Inter-House Competition*

We should organise our work systematically. The diagram below displays clearly the number of games played

	A	B	C	D
A		★	★	★
B			★	★
C				★
D				

The number of games played is $3 + 2 + 1 = 6$.

Now to investigate further. Let us consider five teams in the competition.

	A	B	C	D	E
A		★	★	★	★
B			★	★	★
C				★	★
D					★
E					

Clearly with five teams the number of games played is $4 + 3 + 2 + 1 = 10$. By setting out our work systematically, it has already become apparent that with twelve teams in the competition there would have to be

$11 + 10 + 9 + 8 + 7 + 6 + 5 + 4 + 3 + 2 + 1 = 66$ games played.

When asked to investigate further, the student should realise that he is expected to find the number of games played if there were n teams in the competition.

With n teams the number of games to be played is
$(n-1) + (n-2) + (n-3) + \ldots + 3 + 2 + 1.$

We saw in Chapter 1 how to evaluate this.

  sum $= (n-1) + (n-2) + (n-3) + \ldots + 3 + 2 + 1$ ——①
also, sum $= 1 + 2 + 3 + \ldots + (n-3) + (n-2) + (n-1)$ ——②

Adding gives

  twice sum $= n + n + n + \ldots + n + n + n$ to $(n-1)$ terms.

Hence twice sum $= n(n-1)$

and so   sum $= \frac{n}{2}(n-1)$

i.e. with n teams in the competition, the number of games played is $\frac{n}{2}(n-1)$.

To test our conjecture, we shall let the number of teams, $n = 6$.

Number of games played would be $\frac{6}{2}(6-1) = 15$ which is correct according to our table below, which follows a pattern of triangular numbers.

Number of teams	1	2	3	4	5	6	12	n
Number of games	0	1	3	6	10	15	66	$\frac{n}{2}(n-1)$

The competition, with twelve teams competing, requires 66 games to be played.

Solution to Investigation 11: *Football Leagues*

Again we do not charge into the problem in an attempt to list every game played by every team.

We shall consider simpler but similar situations first and organise our results systematically.

Consider first a league consisting of only two teams, e.g. Aberdeen and Motherwell.

We shall present our work in a table.

	Home Team	
	A	M
A	(A, A)	(M, A)
M	(A, M)	(M, M)

(Away Team)

Clearly, Aberdeen will not play against Aberdeen and Motherwell will not play against Motherwell and so the diagonal of the table should be scored out.

With two teams the total number of games played would be 2.

Now let us consider a league consisting of three teams, e.g. Aberdeen, Motherwell and Hibernian.

		Home Team		
		A	M	H
A w a y T e a m	A	~~(A, A)~~	(M, A)	(H, A)
	M	(A, M)	~~(M, M)~~	(H, M)
	H	(A, H)	(M, H)	~~(H, H)~~

And so the diagonal of the table has been *scored out*.

With three teams in the league, the number of games played would be 6.

The student should now complete the table below, which is constructed for four teams, Aberdeen, Motherwell, Hibernian and Rangers.

		Home Team			
		A	M	H	R
A w a y T e a m	A	~~(A, A)~~	(M, A)	(H, A)	(R, A)
	M	(A, M)	~~(M, M)~~	(H, M)	...
	H	(A, H)	(M, H)	~~(H, H)~~	...
	R	(A, R)	(M, R)	(H, R)	...

With four teams, the number of games would be 12.

Perhaps by this time the number of games played when we have a league consisting of five teams could be deduced. It is left for the reader to complete the table set out below for five teams, Aberdeen, Motherwell, Hibernian, Rangers and Celtic.

		Home Team				
		A	M	H	R	C
A w a y T e a m	A					
	M					
	H					
	R					
	C					

The number of games played when five teams are involved would be 20, i.e. a 5×5 grid minus the number in the diagonal, 5.

Conclusion:

It appears that if we have a league consisting of n teams then the number of games played should be $n \times n - n$ or $n^2 - n$.

With the Premier League consisting of ten teams during season 1990–91, the number of games played should be $10^2 - 10 = 100 - 10 = 90$.

This time our conjecture could be tested by analysing our results and by trying to detect a pattern, from the number of teams and the number of games played.

Number of teams	1	2	3	4	5	10	n
Number of games	0	2	6	12	20	90	

The information does produce a pattern which becomes clearer when displayed as follows:

Number of teams	Number of games
2	$1 \times 2 = 2$
3	$2 \times 3 = 6$
4	$3 \times 4 = 12$
5	$4 \times 5 = 20$
.	
.	
.	
10	$9 \times 10 = 90$
.	
.	
.	
n	$(n-1) \times n = n^2 - n$

This is the result which we noted earlier.

It should be pointed out, however, that every team in the Scottish Premier League plays every other team **twice** at home and **twice** away and so the total number of games played during season 1990–91 was not 90 but 180.

Solution to Investigation 12: *Restructured Football League*

Using the information learned from the previous investigation, if n is the number of teams and g represents the number of games to be played then

$$g = n(n-1)$$

with 10 teams, $\quad g = 10(10-1) = 10(9) = 90$
with 12 teams, $\quad g = 12(12-1) = 12(11) = 132$
and so the difference is $132 - 90 = 42$.

Conclusion:

As every team plays every other team twice at home and twice away, the addition of two extra teams to the league resulted in 42×2, i.e. 84 more, games having to be played.

6. Investigating with Circles

This section includes a number of investigations concerning the circumference of a circle and the area of a circle.

For example, we used the Theorem of Pythagoras which states that 'the **square** on the hypotenuse of a right-angled triangle is equal to the sum of the **squares** on the other two sides'.

Jamieson's theorem states that 'the **semi-circle** on the hypotenuse of **any** right-angled triangle is equal to the sum of the **semi-circle** on the other two sides'.

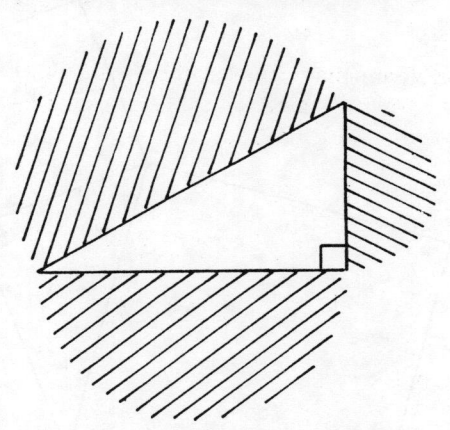

Investigate the truth of this

Investigation 13: *Yan*

Calculate the perimeter of the figure below, given that diameter PR = 10 cm.

You do have enough information

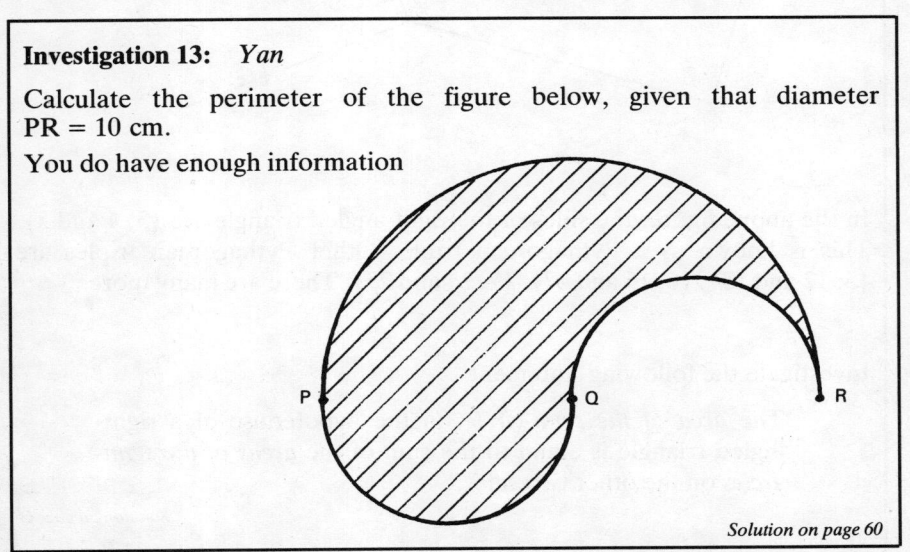

Solution on page 60

Investigation 14:   *The Semi-Circle on the Hypotenuse*

Pythagoras' Theorem states that the *area of the square* on the hypotenuse of a right-angled triangle is equal to the sum of the *areas of the squares* on the other two sides.

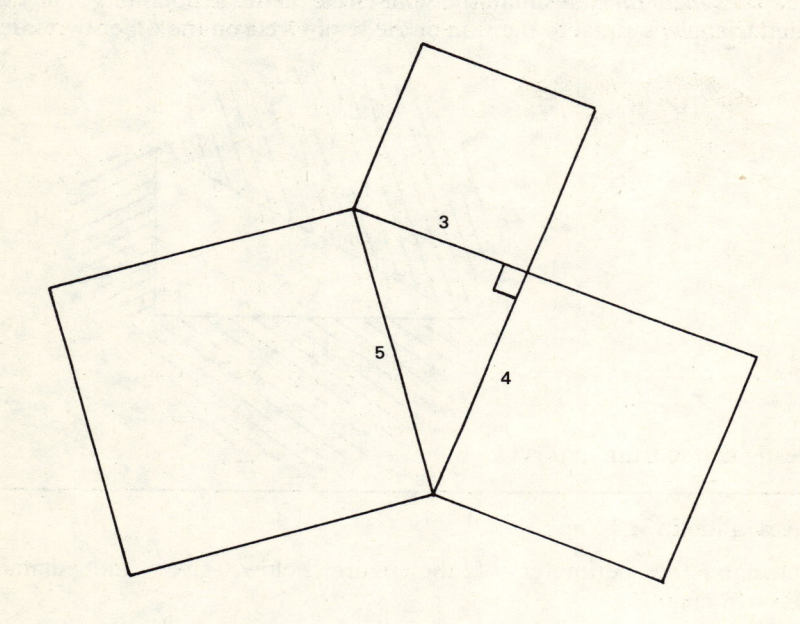

In the above figure, the sides of the right-angled triangle are {3, 4 and 5}. This is known as a Pythagorean triple. Other Pythagorean triples are {5, 12 and 13}, {8, 15 and 17}, {7, 24 and 25}. There are many more.

Investigate the following statement

> 'The *area of the semi-circle* on the hypotenuse of a right-angled triangle is equal to the sum of the *areas of the semi-circles* on the other two sides.'

Solution on page 66

Investigation 15: *Rottweiler*

A rottweiler is tied with a chain 5 metres long to one corner of his kennel, the base of which measures 4 metres by 3 metres. Find the **exact** area within which the rottweiler may stray.

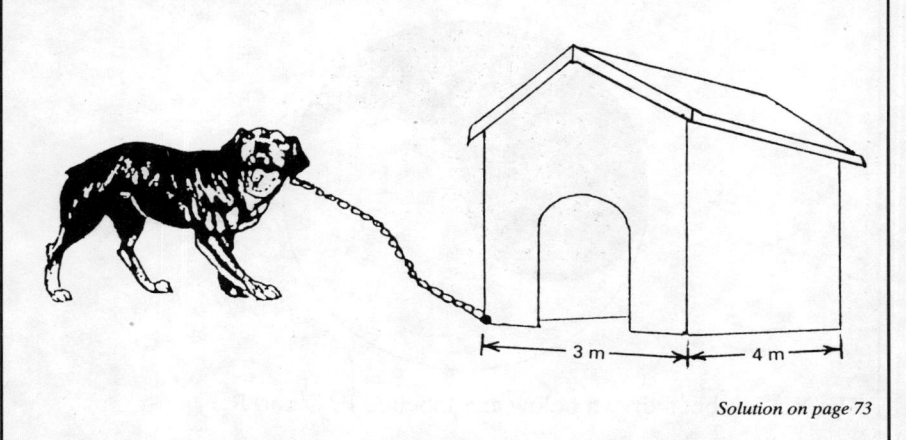

Solution on page 73

Investigation 16: *Big Yin*

The symbol below is part of the Korean ensign. The two parts into which the circle is divided are known as the Yin and the Yan — to many orientals they represent the eternal male and female forces of nature.

The Yin has been drawn below and labelled P, Q and R.

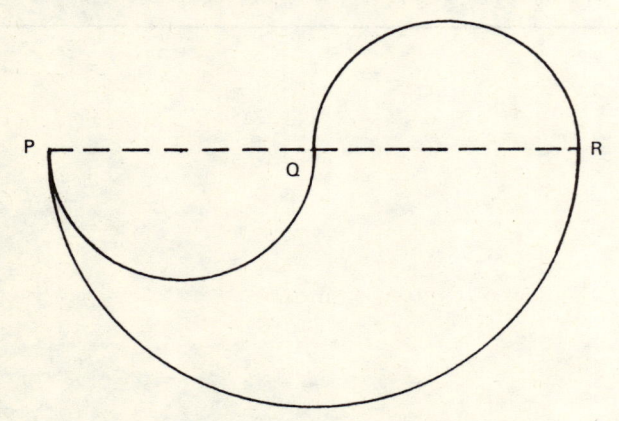

(a) In the above diagram Q is the mid-point of PR, which is 16 cm long. Draw the figure accurately and calculate its **exact** area.

(b) **Investigate** the area of the Yin for different positions of Q.

Solution on page 73

A **circle** is defined to be the set of all the points in a plane which are equidistant from a fixed point, the centre. The distance from these points to the centre is known as the radius.

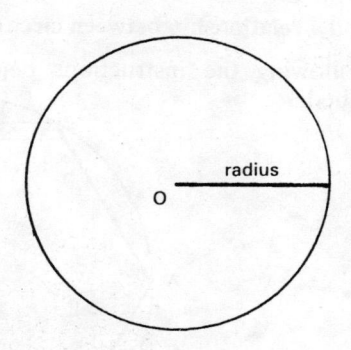

The **circumference** of a circle is the distance around the circle. Circumference is another name for the perimeter of a circle.

The **diameter** of a circle is a line which joins any two points on the circumference and passes through the centre of the circle.

The diameter is twice the length of the radius.

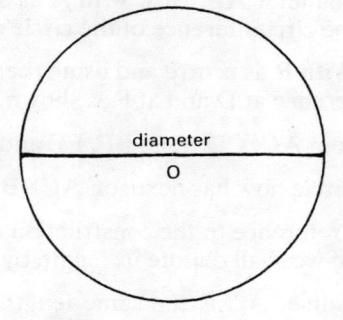

An **arc** of a circle is a part of the circumference.

53

To find a relationship between circumference and diameter

By following the instructions below, construct a circle with a hexagon inscribed.

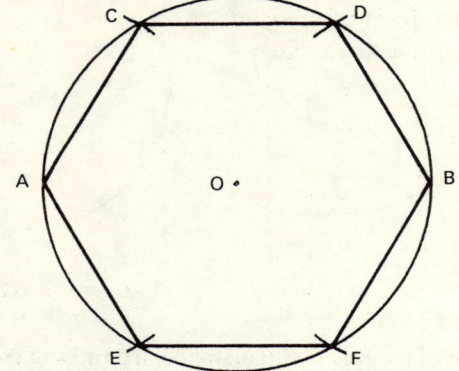

(a) Draw a circle of any suitable radius. Find the centre O, and draw any diameter AB. Now with A as centre and AO as radius, draw arcs cutting the circumference of the circle at C and E as shown.

(b) With B as centre and using the same radius, draw arcs cutting the circumference at D and at F as shown.

(c) Join AC, CD, DB, BF, FE and EA.

The circle now has hexagon ACDBFE inscribed.

With reference to the construction above, the diameter AB is twice the radius and so we shall denote its length by $2r$.

Of course, AC is the same length as the radius AO. The perimeter of the hexagon must therefore be $6r$.

Hence the perimeter of the hexagon is equal to three times the length of the diameter.

It is clear that the circumference of the circle is greater than the perimeter of the hexagon and so we may conclude that the circumference of a circle, C, is more than three times the length of the diameter, d.

The following interesting biblical quotation which refers to the building of King Solomon's palaces indicates that the people of his time understood that the circumference of a circle was approximately three times the diameter.

> 1 KINGS, Chapter 7, verse 23
> "And he made a molten sea, **ten** cubits from one brim to the other: it was round all about, and his height was five cubits: and a line of **thirty** cubits did encompass it round about."

In fact, the ratio of the circumference of any circle to its diameter is just more than 3; it is the value π (pi).

$$\frac{\text{circumference}}{\text{diameter}} = \pi \quad \text{or} \quad C = \pi \times d$$

$\pi = 3$ (to 1 significant figure)
$\pi = 3\cdot1$ (to 2 significant figures)
$\pi = 3\cdot14$ (to 3 significant figures)
$\pi = 3\cdot142$ (to 4 significant figures)
$\pi = 3\cdot1415$ (to 5 significant figures)
$\pi = 3\cdot14159$ (to 6 significant figures).

In fact, π is an irrational number, i.e. a number which when expressed as a decimal does not have an exact value; it does not terminate or recur.

$\pi = 3\cdot141\ 592\ 653\ 589\ 793\ \ldots$ (omitting the next 499,975 places) $\ldots$ 513 819 524 2 $\ldots$

It should be made clear to the student that π is **not** equal to the fraction $\frac{22}{7}$. This fraction is merely an approximation for π which, when expressed as a decimal, is $3\cdot142\ 857\ 1\ \ldots$ which is **not** π.

Since π is an irrational number there is no fraction to which it is exactly equal. However, a better fractional approximation to π than $\frac{22}{7}$ is the fraction $\frac{355}{113}$. It is left as an exercise for the student to find how many decimal places this fraction compares with π.

Example 1

Calculate the circumference of the circle in the diagram below.

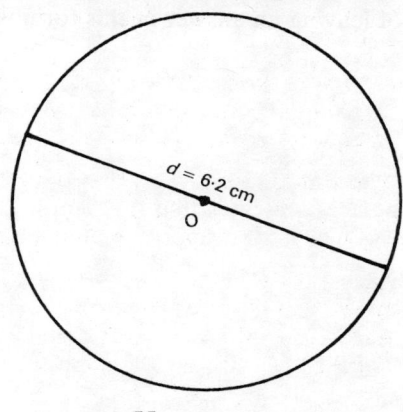

$C = \pi \times d$
$C = \pi \times 6\cdot2$
$C = 19\cdot477\,874\,45 \ldots$ units.

We must now decide how to give our answer.

As the original measurement was given to 2 significant figures, i.e. 6·2 units, we are entitled to give our answer to no more than the same number of significant figures, i.e. 2.

It would be wrong to give the length of the circumference as 19·477 874 45 . . .

The length of the circumference should be given as 19 units (to 2 significant figures).

It is common in mathematical calculations involving the circle to leave an answer as a multiple of π.

Example 2

Find the circumference of the circle which as a radius of 7 cm.

$C = \pi \times d$
$C = \pi \times 14$ (since diameter = twice the radius)
$C = 14\pi$ cm.

The advantage of leaving an answer in this form is that it is exact and not an approximation.

Example 3

Copy the figure below using the measurements stated. Calculate the perimeter of the figure.

PR = 4 inches
PQ = 2 inches

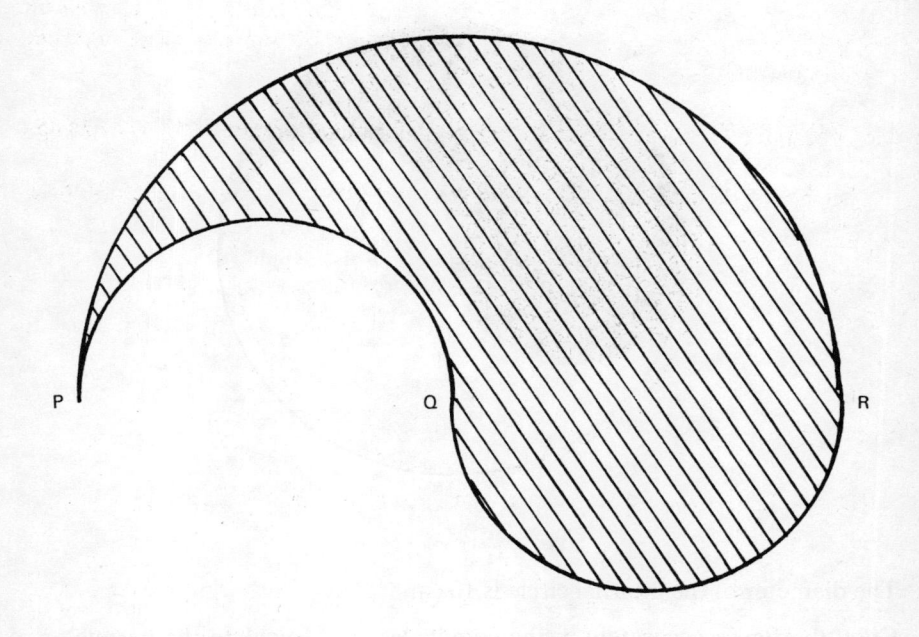

Perimeter of semi-circle PR $= \frac{1}{2} \times \pi \times d = \frac{1}{2} \times \pi \times 4 = 2\pi$ inches.

Perimeter of semi-circle PQ $= \frac{1}{2} \times \pi \times d = \frac{1}{2} \times \pi \times 2 = \pi$ inches.

Perimeter of semi-circle QR $= \frac{1}{2} \times \pi \times d = \frac{1}{2} \times \pi \times 2 = \pi$ inches.

Hence the total perimeter of the figure $= 4\pi$ inches.

Example 4   The Great Monad

The symbol illustrated below is displayed on the South Korean flag and is known as the Great Monad. To many easterners this symbol represents eternity. The two parts into which the circle is divided are called *yin* and *yan* — the male and female forces of nature.

The diameter of the internal circle is 10 cm.

Copy the figure accurately, using compasses, and calculate the perimeter of the *yan*, the shaded portion.

Solution:

The perimeter of the *yan* is 10π cm.

Example 5 The Underground

The diagram below illustrates the layout of an underground railway network.

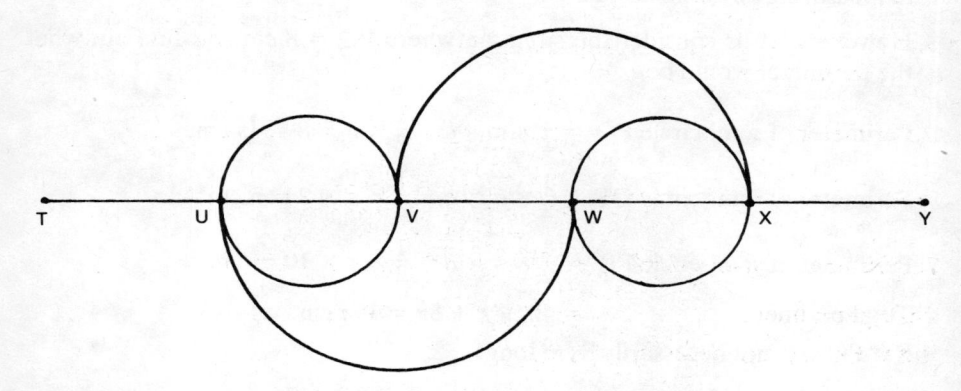

If the shortest distance between each neighbouring station is equal to 1 km, calculate the shortest and longest distance from T to Y.

Solution:

T → U → V → W → X → Y in a straight line is 5 km.

Now consider the route, line TU, semi-circle UV, semi-circle VX, line XY, which appears to be the longest route.

Line TU = 1 km

semi-circle UV = $\frac{1}{2} \times \pi \times d = \frac{1}{2} \times \pi \times 1 = \frac{1}{2}\pi$ km.

semi-circle VX = $\frac{1}{2} \times \pi \times d = \frac{1}{2} \times \pi \times 2 = \pi$ km.

line XY = 1 km.

Longest distance from T to Y = $1 + \frac{1}{2}\pi + \pi + 1 = 2 + \frac{3}{2}\pi$ km.

The student should complete the problem by showing that no other route is longer than this one.

Solution to Investigation 13: *Yan*

The diagram on page 49 has not been drawn to scale and so there is no point in measuring any dimensions.

However, let us consider the situation where PQ = 8 cm and find out what the perimeter would be.

Perimeter of semi-circle PQ $= \frac{1}{2} \times \pi \times d = \frac{1}{2} \times \pi \times 8 = 4\pi$ cm.

Perimeter of semi-circle QR $= \frac{1}{2} \times \pi \times d = \frac{1}{2} \times \pi \times 2 = \pi$ cm.

Perimeter of semi-circle PR $= \frac{1}{2} \times \pi \times d = \frac{1}{2} \times \pi \times 10 = 5\pi$ cm.

Total perimeter $= 4\pi + \pi + 5\pi = 10\pi$ cm.

But PQ was not necessarily 8 cm long.

Let us now see what answer we would obtain if PQ = 7 cm.

Perimeter of semi-circle PQ $= \frac{1}{2} \times \pi \times d = \frac{1}{2} \times \pi \times 7 = 3\frac{1}{2}\pi$ cm.

Perimeter of semi-circle QR $= \frac{1}{2} \times \pi \times d = \frac{1}{2} \times \pi \times 3 = 1\frac{1}{2}\pi$ cm.

Perimeter of semi-circle PR $= \frac{1}{2} \times \pi \times d = \frac{1}{2} \times \pi \times 10 = 5\pi$ cm.

Total perimeter $= 3\frac{1}{2}\pi + 1\frac{1}{2}\pi + 5\pi = 10\pi$ cm.

Again the perimeter is 10π. We must check to see if this is coincidental.

What would the perimeter be if PQ = 6 cm?

Perimeter of semi-circle PQ $= \frac{1}{2} \times \pi \times d = \frac{1}{2} \times \pi \times 6 = 3\pi$ cm.

Perimeter of semi-circle QR $= \frac{1}{2} \times \pi \times d = \frac{1}{2} \times \pi \times 4 = 2\pi$ cm.

Perimeter of semi-circle PR $= \frac{1}{2} \times \pi \times d = \frac{1}{2} \times \pi \times 10 = 5\pi$ cm.

Total perimeter $= 3\pi + 2\pi + 5\pi = 10\pi$ cm.

Again the total perimeter is 10π.

We will carry out one more calculation, i.e. where Q is the mid-point of PR.

Perimeter of semi-circle PQ $= \frac{1}{2} \times \pi \times d = \frac{1}{2} \times \pi \times 5 = 2\frac{1}{2}\pi$ cm.

Perimeter of semi-circle QR $= \frac{1}{2} \times \pi \times d = \frac{1}{2} \times \pi \times 5 = 2\frac{1}{2}\pi$ cm.

Perimeter of semi-circle PR $= \frac{1}{2} \times \pi \times d = \frac{1}{2} \times \pi \times 10 = 5\pi$ cm.

Total perimeter $= 2\frac{1}{2}\pi + 2\frac{1}{2}\pi + 5\pi = 10\pi$ cm.

It appears that no matter the position of Q the perimeter is 10π cm.

The following approach to this investigation is a more sophisticated one.

What would the perimeter be if PQ $= a$ cm (i.e. any length)?

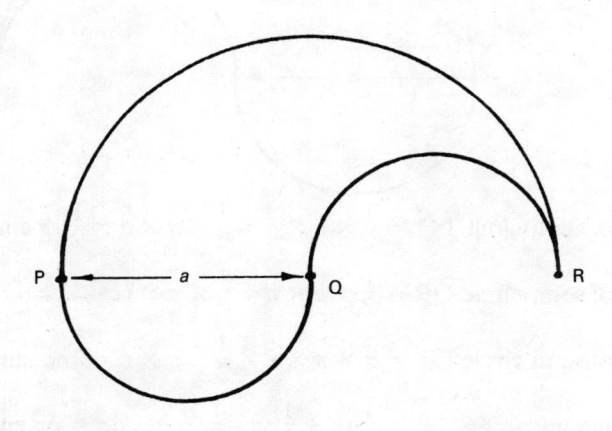

Perimeter of semi-circle PQ $= \frac{1}{2} \times \pi \times d = \frac{1}{2} \times \pi \times a = \frac{1}{2}a\pi$ cm.

Perimeter of semi-circle QR $= \frac{1}{2} \times \pi \times d = \frac{1}{2} \times \pi \times (10-a) = 5\pi - \frac{1}{2}a\pi$ cm.

Perimeter of semi-circle PR $= \frac{1}{2} \times \pi \times d = \frac{1}{2} \times \pi \times 10 = 5\pi$ cm.

Total perimeter $= \frac{1}{2}a\pi + 5\pi - \frac{1}{2}a\pi + 5\pi = 10\pi$ cm.

Conclusion:

This argument proves that whatever the position of Q the perimeter of the *yan* is 10π cm.

Taking the investigation further — perhaps there is a connection between the length of any *yan* and its perimeter.

In the figure below the length of diameter PR is c cm this time instead of 10 cm as before. PQ = a cm.

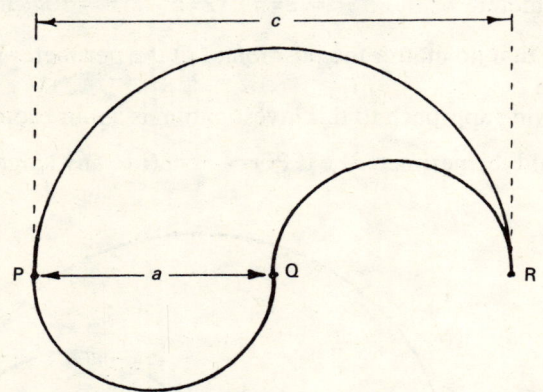

Perimeter of semi-circle PQ $= \frac{1}{2} \times \pi \times d = \frac{1}{2} \times \pi \times a = \frac{1}{2} a \pi$ cm.

Perimeter of semi-circle QR $= \frac{1}{2} \times \pi \times d = \frac{1}{2} \times \pi \times (c - a) = \frac{1}{2} c \pi - \frac{1}{2} a \pi$ cm.

Perimeter of semi-circle PR $= \frac{1}{2} \times \pi \times d = \frac{1}{2} \times \pi \times c = \frac{1}{2} c \pi$ cm.

Total perimeter $= \frac{1}{2} a \pi + \frac{1}{2} c \pi - \frac{1}{2} a \pi + \frac{1}{2} c \pi = c \pi$ cm.

Conclusion:

This argument shows that the perimeter of the *yan* is related to its length; if the length is c units then the perimeter is $c \times \pi$ units.

Construction:

The student should complete this section on semi-circles by doing the following construction, which shows how to divide a circle into any number of parts equal in perimeter.

Draw a diameter AB and divide it into as many equal parts as the circle is to have divisions (in this illustration 3).

On A1 and A2 draw the semi-circles *a* and *b*.

On B1 and B2 draw the semi-circles *c* and *d*.

The circle is now divided into three parts. The student should prove that these three parts are equal in perimeter.

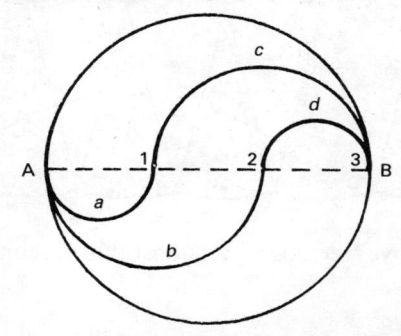

As a further exercise, the student should carry out the construction to divide a given circle into four parts, equal in perimeter.

Area of a Circle

The circle below has been divided into twelve equal slices or *sectors*.

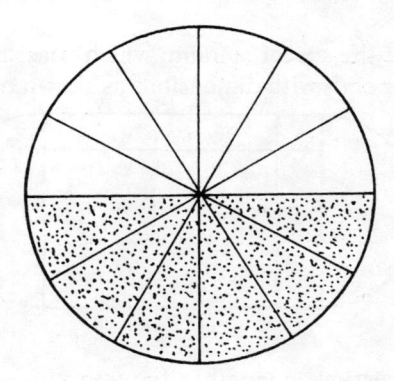

If we now cut out the sectors and place them side by side, as shown, we have a shape which resembles a rectangle. Notice that one of the sectors has been bisected (cut in two equal parts) and each part has been added to either end of the figure.

The more sectors that are taken in this rearrangement of the circle, the more the newly formed figure would resemble a rectangle.

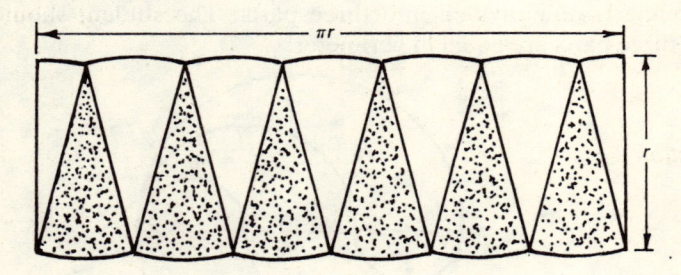

The length of the above 'rectangle' is half of the circumference, i.e. $\frac{1}{2}$ of $\pi d =$ $\frac{1}{2} \times \pi \times 2r = \pi \times r$.

The breadth of the 'rectangle' $= r$.

The area of the 'rectangle' $=$ length $\times$ breadth $= \pi \times r \times r = \pi r^2$.

It follows that **the area of the circle, with radius r, may be found by the formula, $A = \pi r^2$.**

Question 1

Calculate the area of the soccer stadium which consists of a rectangular area and two semi-circular ends with dimensions as shown below.

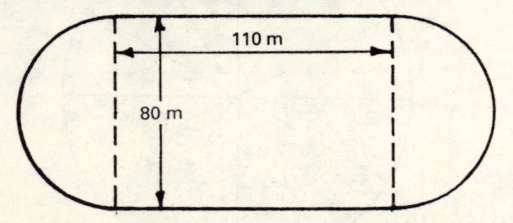

Solution:

Area of rectangular section = length × breadth
= 110 m × 80 m
= 8 800 m²

Area of circle (i.e. two semi-circles) $= \pi r^2$
$= \pi \times 40^2$
$= 1600\pi \text{ m}^2$
$= 5026 \cdot 5482 \ldots \text{ m}^2$
$= 5000 \text{ m}^2$ (to 2 significant figures)

Total area of soccer stadium $= 8800 + 5000 = 13\,800 \text{ m}^2$

Question 2

A wooden beam of square cross section of side 44 cm is cut from a cylindrical log. Calculate the diameter of the log and the area of the circular cross-section of the log.

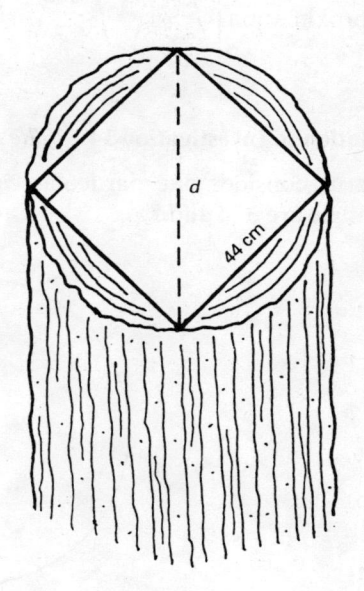

Solution:

We find the diameter using Pythagoras' Theorem.

$d^2 = 44^2 + 44^2$
$d^2 = 1936 + 1936$
$d^2 = 3872$
$d = \sqrt{3872}$
$d = 62$ (to 2 significant figures)

Hence diameter = 62 cm.

Now to find the area of the circle using radius $r = 31$ cm (half of the diameter).

$$\begin{aligned}\text{Area} &= \pi r^2 \\ &= \pi \times 31^2 \\ &= \pi \times 961 \\ &= 3019 \cdot 0705 \ldots \\ &= 3000 \text{ cm}^2 \quad \text{(to 2 significant figures)}\end{aligned}$$

Hence area of the log's circular cross section is 3000 cm^2. Of course, no tree would have a true circular cross-section and so the answer is an approximation.

Solution to Investigation 14: *The Semi-Circle on the Hypotenuse*

Let us consider one particular case in which the sides of the right-angled triangle are 3, 4 and 5.

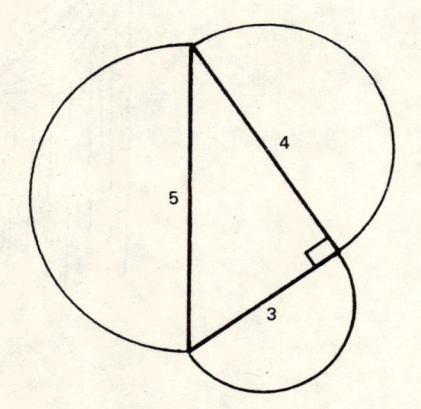

Area of the semi-circle on the hypotenuse $= \frac{1}{2}\pi r^2 = \frac{1}{2}\pi \times 2 \cdot 5^2$

$\qquad\qquad\qquad\qquad\qquad\qquad\qquad = 3 \cdot 125\pi$ units^2

Area of the semi-circle on the smallest side $= \frac{1}{2}\pi r^2 = \frac{1}{2}\pi \times 1 \cdot 5^2$

$\qquad\qquad\qquad\qquad\qquad\qquad\qquad = 1 \cdot 125\pi$ units^2

Area of the semi-circle on the second side $= \frac{1}{2}\pi r^2 = \frac{1}{2}\pi \times 2^2$

$\qquad\qquad\qquad\qquad\qquad\qquad\qquad\quad = 2\pi$ units^2

And so, with lengths of sides 3, 4 and 5, the areas of the semi-circles on the other two sides $= 2\pi + 1 \cdot 125\pi = 3 \cdot 125\pi = $ the area of the semi-circle on the hypotenuse.

This does not prove that the given statement is true for **every** right-angled triangle but only for those of sides 3, 4 and 5 units.

Before we generalise, it may be worth investigating with right-angled triangles whose sides are made up of some of the Pythagorean triples mentioned on page 50.

With sides 5, 12 and 13

Area of the semi-circle on the hypotenuse $= \frac{1}{2}\pi r^2 = \frac{1}{2}\pi \times 6.5^2$

$\qquad\qquad\qquad\qquad\qquad\qquad\qquad\quad = 21 \cdot 125\pi$ units^2

Area of the semi-circle on the smallest side $= \frac{1}{2}\pi r^2 = \frac{1}{2}\pi \times 2.5^2$

$\qquad\qquad\qquad\qquad\qquad\qquad\qquad\quad = 3 \cdot 125\pi$ units^2

Area of the semi-circle on the second side $= \frac{1}{2}\pi r^2 = \frac{1}{2}\pi \times 6^2$

$\qquad\qquad\qquad\qquad\qquad\qquad\qquad\quad = 18\pi$ units^2

And so with lengths of sides 5, 12 and 13 the areas of the semi-circles on the other two sides $= 18\pi + 3 \cdot 125\pi = 21 \cdot 125\pi = $ the area of the semi-circle on the hypotenuse.

This does not prove that the given statement is true for **every** right-angled triangle.

Let us now try the same calculation for a right-angled triangle with sides of length **8, 15 and 17**.

Area of the semi-circle on the hypotenuse $= \frac{1}{2}\pi r^2 = \frac{1}{2}\pi \times 8.5^2$

$\qquad\qquad\qquad\qquad\qquad\qquad\qquad\quad = 36 \cdot 125\pi$ units^2

Area of the semi-circle on the smallest side $= \frac{1}{2}\pi r^2 = \frac{1}{2}\pi \times 4^2$

$\qquad\qquad\qquad\qquad\qquad\qquad\qquad\quad = 8\pi$ units^2

Area of the semi-circle on the second side $= \frac{1}{2}\pi r^2 = \frac{1}{2}\pi \times 7\cdot 5^2$

$\qquad\qquad\qquad\qquad\qquad\qquad\qquad\quad = 28\cdot 125\pi$ units^2

And so with lengths of sides 8, 15 and 17 the areas of the semi-circles on the other two sides $= 28\cdot 125\pi + 8\pi = 36\cdot 125\pi =$ the area of the semi-circle on the hypotenuse.

This does not prove that the given statement is true for **every** right-angled triangle, although it is looking increasingly likely.

To prove that 'the *area of the semi-circle* on the hypotenuse of **every** right-angled triangle is equal to the sum of the *areas of the semi-circles* on the other two sides', we must use letters to generalise the result.

Let the sides have lengths a, b and c where a is the length of the hypotenuse. Then $a^2 = b^2 + c^2$.

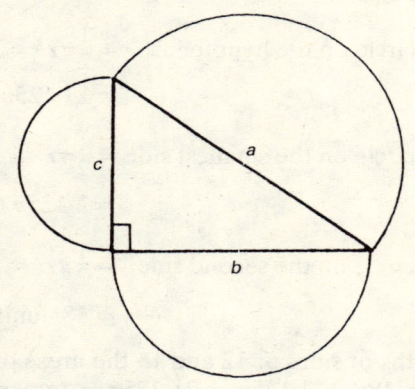

Area of the semi-circle on the hypotenuse $= \frac{1}{2}\pi r^2 = \frac{1}{2}\pi \times \left(\frac{1}{2}a\right)^2$

$\qquad\qquad\qquad\qquad\qquad\qquad\qquad\quad = \frac{1}{8}a^2\pi$ units^2

Area of the semi-circle on the smallest side $= \frac{1}{2}\pi r^2 = \frac{1}{2}\pi \times \left(\frac{1}{2}c\right)^2$

$\qquad\qquad\qquad\qquad\qquad\qquad\qquad\quad = \frac{1}{8}c^2\pi$ units^2

Area of the semi-circle on the second side $= \frac{1}{2}\pi r^2 = \frac{1}{2}\pi \times \left(\frac{1}{2}b\right)^2$

$\qquad\qquad\qquad\qquad\qquad\qquad\qquad\quad = \frac{1}{8}b^2\pi$ units^2

Hence the sum of the areas of the semi-circles on the other two sides

$= \frac{1}{8}c^2\pi + \frac{1}{8}b^2\pi$

$= \frac{1}{8}\pi(c^2 + b^2)$

$= \frac{1}{8}\pi a^2 \quad$ since $a^2 = b^2 + c^2$

$=$ area of the semi-circle on the hypotenuse.

This argument proves that the given statement is true for **any** right-angled triangle.

Question:

Calculate the area shaded in the diagram below.

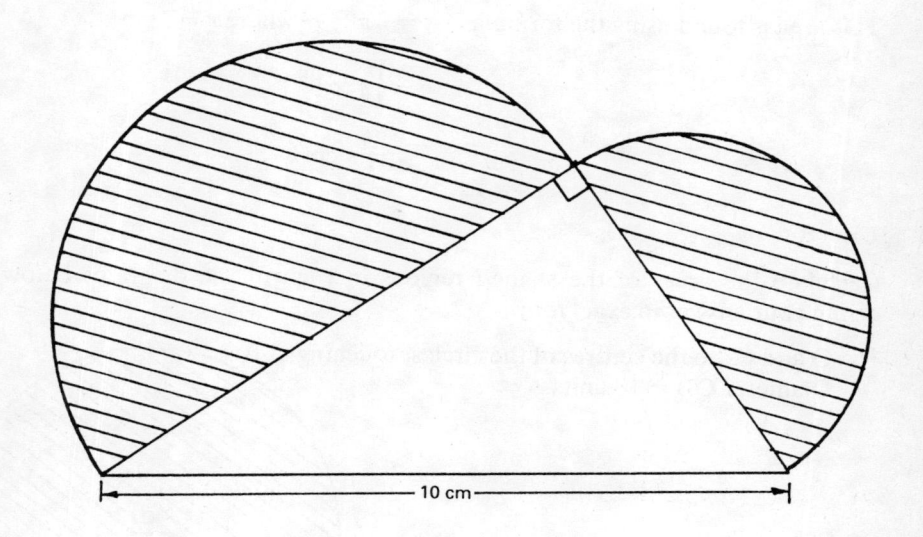

We have just proved that the Theorem of Pythagoras may be extended to semi-circles, i.e. **the area of the semi-circle on the hypotenuse of a right-angled triangle = the sum of the areas of the semi-circles on the other two sides.**

Hence the required area in the diagram on the previous page is equivalent to the area shaded in the diagram below.

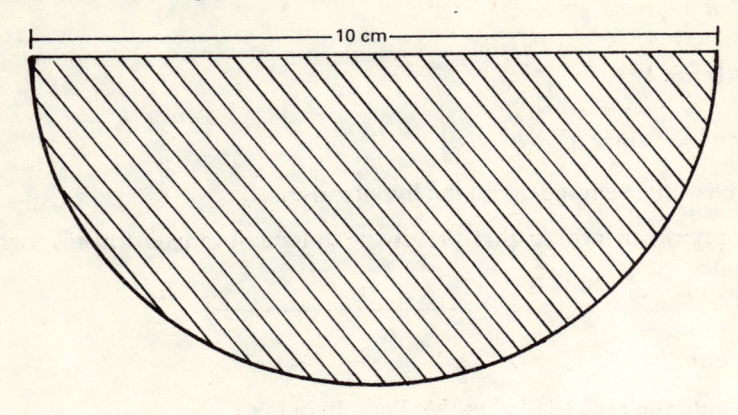

This area is found using the formula $A = \frac{1}{2}\pi \times r^2$ where $r = 5$ cm

$$= \frac{1}{2}\pi \times 5^2$$

$$= \frac{25}{2}\pi \text{ cm}^2$$

Exercise:

Calculate the areas of the shaded regions in each of the diagrams below, giving your answer in **exact** form.

1. O and C are the centres of the circles, touching at B. Diameter OB = 10 units.

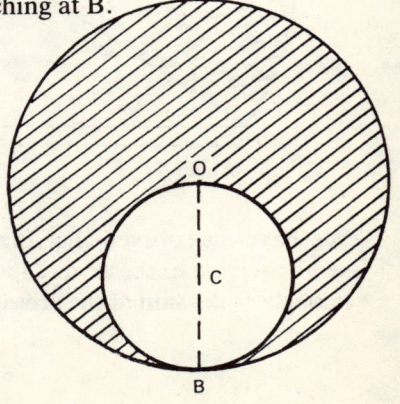

2. PQRS is a square. The enclosed circle, with radius 6 units and centre C, touches the sides of the square.

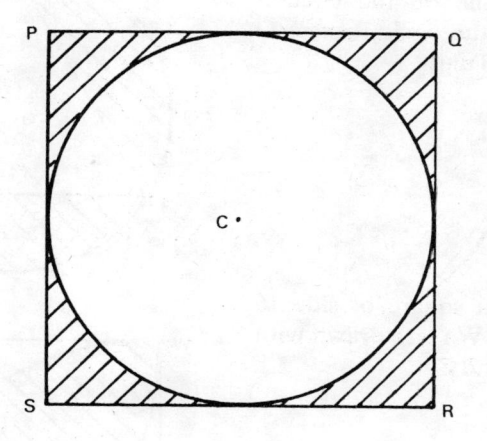

3. TUVW is a square with T, U, V, W on the circumference of the circle, centre C. Diameter of the circle is 50 cm.

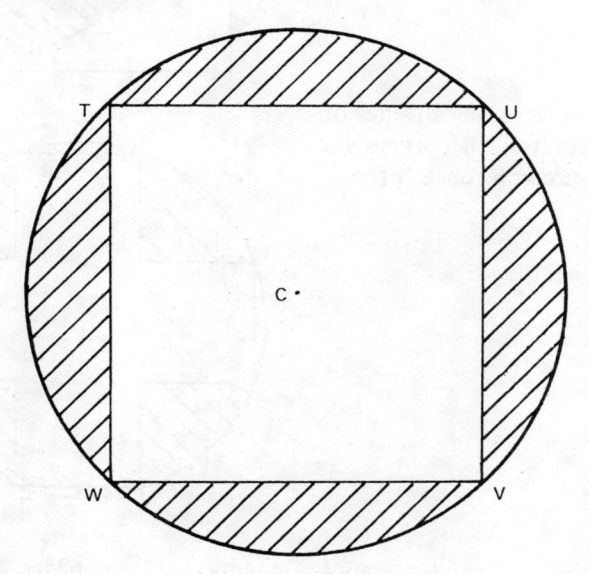

4. Triangle ABC is equilateral, i.e. all sides are equal. A, B and C all lie on the circumference of the circle, centre O and radius 8 units.

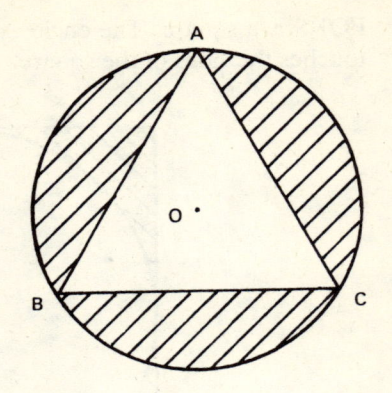

5. WXYZ is a square of side 16 units. Arcs WY are drawn with centres X and Z.

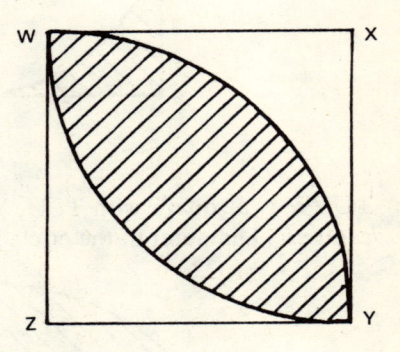

6. The Greek cross has all sides of length 4 units. All corners lie on the circumference of the circle.

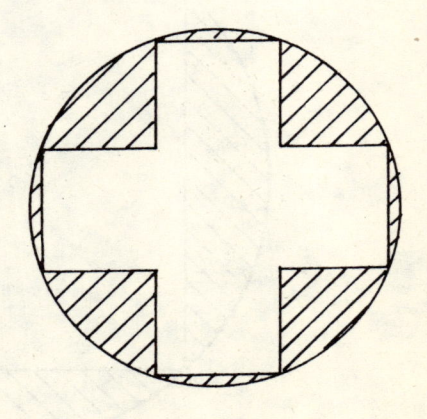

Solutions:
1. 75π units^2
2. $36(4-\pi)$ units^2
3. $625(\pi-2)$ cm^2
4. $16(4\pi - 3\sqrt{3})$ units^2
5. $128(\pi-2)$ units^2
6. $40(\pi-2)$ units^2

Solution to Investigation 15: *Rottweiler*

To understand the problem better we should produce a sketch. Perhaps a diagram drawn to scale would be useful.

Setting the radius of our compasses to the length of the rottweiler's chain, i.e. 5 units, and placing the point of the compasses at one corner of the kennel 4 units by 3 units, we can clearly see the area to be calculated.

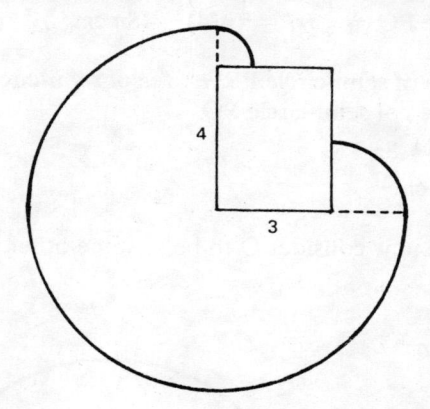

The area consists of three parts, i.e. one $\frac{3}{4}$ circle and two $\frac{1}{4}$ circles.

It is now left as an exercise for the student to complete the investigation by proving that the total area available to the rottweiler is 20π metres^2.

Solution to Investigation 16: *Big Yin*

(a) Using compasses and correct radii, we draw the figure to as high a degree of accuracy as possible.

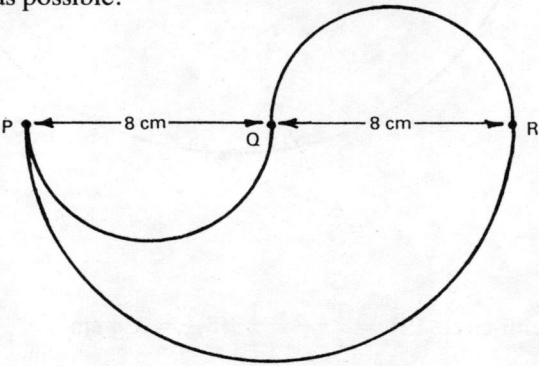

Where Q is the mid-point of PR

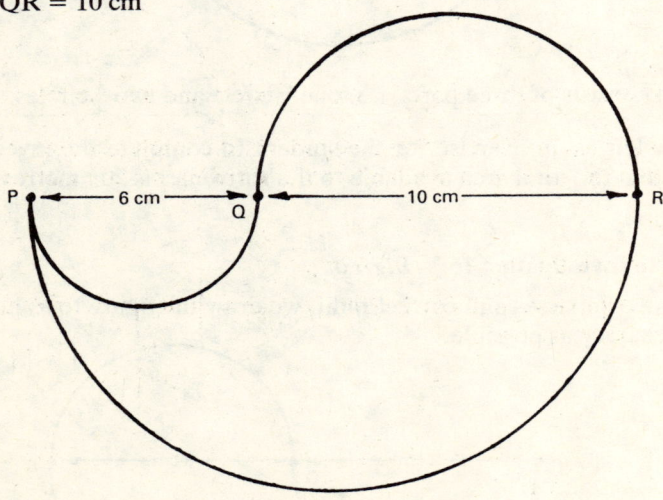

Area of semi-circle PR $= \frac{1}{2}\pi r^2 = \frac{1}{2}\pi(8)^2 = 32\pi$ cm^2

Area of semi-circle QR $= \frac{1}{2}\pi r^2 = \frac{1}{2}\pi(4)^2 = 8\pi$ cm^2

Area of semi-circle PQ $= \frac{1}{2}\pi r^2 = \frac{1}{2}\pi(4)^2 = 8\pi$ cm^2

Area of yin = area of semi-circle PR + area of semi-circle QR
  − area of semi-circle PQ
$= 32\pi + 8\pi - 8\pi$
$= 32\pi$ cm^2

(b) As directed, let us now consider Q to be at some other points on the line QR.
Let PQ = 6 cm
and so QR = 10 cm

Area of semi-circle PR $= \frac{1}{2}\pi r^2 = \frac{1}{2}\pi(8)^2 = 32\pi$ cm^2

Area of semi-circle QR = $\frac{1}{2}\pi r^2 = \frac{1}{2}\pi(5)^2 = 12\frac{1}{2}\pi$ cm²

Area of semi-circle PQ = $\frac{1}{2}\pi r^2 = \frac{1}{2}\pi(3)^2 = 4\frac{1}{2}\pi$ cm²

Area of yin = area of semi-circle PR + area of semi-circle QR
 − area of semi-circle PQ

$= 32\pi + 12\frac{1}{2}\pi - 4\frac{1}{2}\pi$

$= 40\pi$ cm²

Conclusion:

The area of the yin has increased by placing Q closer to P.

This time let PQ = 10 cm
and so QR = 6 cm

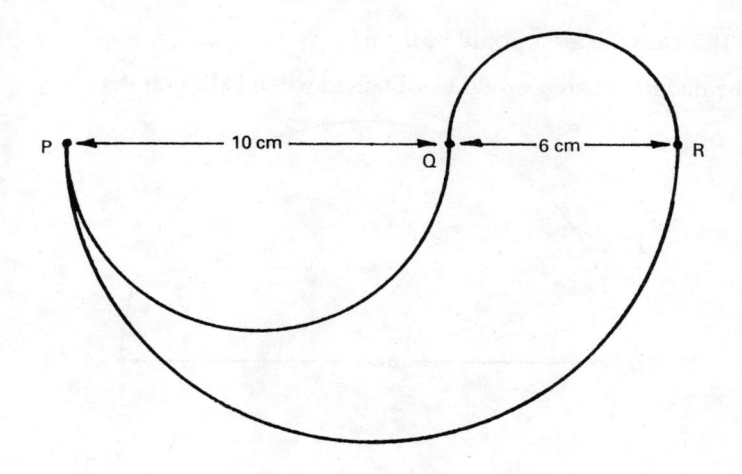

Area of semi-circle PR = $\frac{1}{2}\pi r^2 = \frac{1}{2}\pi(8)^2 = 32\pi$ cm²

Area of semi-circle QR = $\frac{1}{2}\pi r^2 = \frac{1}{2}\pi(3)^2 = 4\frac{1}{2}\pi$ cm²

Area of semi-circle PQ = $\frac{1}{2}\pi r^2 = \frac{1}{2}\pi(5)^2 = 12\frac{1}{2}\pi$ cm²

Area of yin = area of semi-circle PR + area of semi-circle QR
− area of semi-circle PQ

$$= 32\pi + 4\tfrac{1}{2}\pi - 12\tfrac{1}{2}\pi$$

$$= 24\pi \text{ cm}^2$$

Conclusion:

The area of the yin has increased by placing Q closer to P.

It follows that the minimum area of the figure would be obtained when Q lies on R.

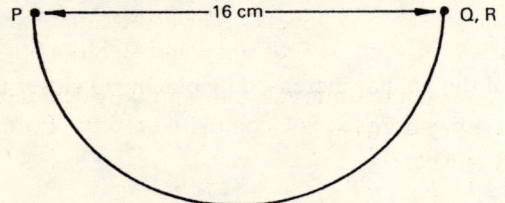

In this case the area would be 0 cm².

The maximum area would be obtained when Q lies on P.

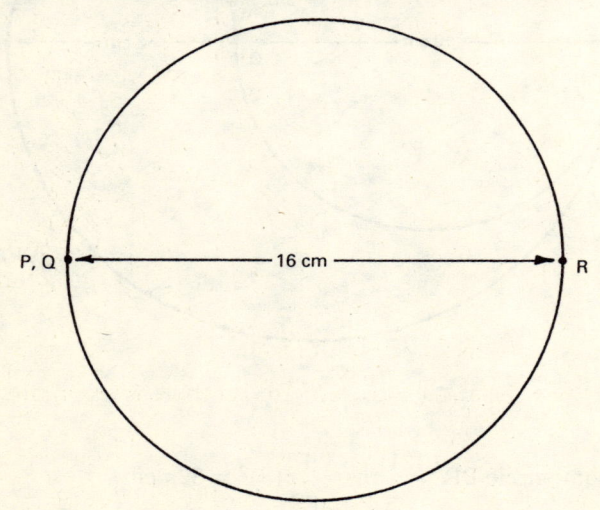

The maximum area would be the area of the circle with radius, $r = \tfrac{1}{2}$PQ.

In the case above, the maximum area would be $\pi(8)^2 = 64\pi$ cm².

7. Solving Problems Using Simultaneous Equations

Investigation 17: *Trees*

The Forestry Commission sells two types of sapling trees to its customers. The two types are Scots Pine and Sitka Spruce.

Five customers each received a bill:

Calculus Castle	:	50 Scots Pine and 40 Sitka Spruce : £160
Erskine Estate	:	100 Scots Pine and 90 Sitka Spruce : £335
Geometric Gardens	:	10 Scots Pine and 80 Sitka Spruce : £125
Haddock House	:	5 Scots Pine and 10 Sitka Spruce : £ 25
Gorky Park	:	60 Scots Pine and 40 Sitka Spruce : £180

The five customers compared their bills and they decided that one of them had been wrongly charged. They complained to the Forestry Commission. Was their claim justified?

Solution on page 83

Simultaneous Equations

The equation $x + y = 8$ has many solutions, e.g. $x = 5$ and $y = 3$ or $x = 1$ and $y = 7$ or $x = 2\frac{1}{2}$ and $y = 5\frac{1}{2}$ etc. In fact there is an infinite number of solutions.

Similarly, the equation $x - y = 4$ has an infinite number of solutions, e.g. $x = 5$ and $y = 1$ or $x = 100$ and $y = 96$ etc.

There is one unique solution which **satisfies** both equations simultaneously, i.e. $x = 6$ and $y = 2$.

Simultaneous equations are equations which have the same solution.

Before attempting any Investigations involving simultaneous equations, first we should ensure that we can readily solve two simultaneous equations.

Although there are numerous methods which can be used for solving simultaneous equations, we shall concentrate on one method only — **the method of elimination**.

Example 1

Let us look again at the two equations above

$$x + y = 8 \quad \text{①}$$
$$x - y = 4 \quad \text{②}$$

Rather than just stare at the two equations and hope that an answer will emerge, we could combine the equations with the object of forming a new equation which involves only one of the unknowns, x or y.

If we add the equations ① and ② together we will **eliminate** the y terms to give $2x = 12$ and $x = 6$ as was suggested earlier. Having found the x value, it is a simple process to find y by substituting 6 in place of x in either of the above equations. Using equation ① gives $6 + y = 8$ and so $y = 2$.

Exercise:

Solve simultaneously the following pairs of equations by adding them, thus eliminating one of the terms, either x or y.

(a) $4x + y = 21$
    $2x - y = 3$

(b) $3x - 2y = 1$
    $-3x + 5y = 20$

Solutions:

(a) $x = 4$ and $y = 5$

(b) $x = 5$ and $y = 7$

Of course, the reader will have realised that this method of elimination works only if there exist two equal terms with opposite signs, one in each equation. When this is not the case it will always be possible to achieve this situation by multiplying each equation by a suitable number.

Example 2

Solve simultaneously the two equations $5x + 2y = 16$
$8x - 3y = 7$

First we should copy and label the two equations

$$5x + 2y = 16 \quad \text{①}$$
$$8x - 3y = 7 \quad \text{②}$$

Here we shall eliminate the y terms by endeavouring to make the y terms equal but opposite in sign. To do this we shall multiply both sides of equation ① by 3 and both sides of equation ② by 2.

The equations will now read
$$15x + 6y = 48 \quad\text{———}\quad ①$$
$$16x - 6y = 14 \quad\text{———}\quad ②$$

We can now add the two equations together as before to eliminate the y terms.

This gives us $\quad 31x = 62$
and so $\quad\quad\quad\quad x = 2$

To find y, we shall substitute this value of x into one of the above original equations. Let us use equation ② this time which will read as
$$16 - 3y = 7$$
and so $\quad\quad\quad 3y = 9$
giving us $\quad\quad y = 3$

We shall finally write the solution as $x = 2$, $y = 3$.

Of course we can check this solution by ensuring that it satisfies equation ①, $5x + 2y = 16$.
$(5 \times 2) + (2 \times 3) = 16$ which is correct.

Exercise:

Using the method illustrated above, solve the following pairs of simultaneous equations.

(a) $4x - 5y = 5$
$\quad\ 2x + \ y = 13$

(b) $4x - \ y = 10$
$\quad\ 3x + 5y = 19$

(c) $9x + 12y = 33$
$\quad\ 8x + 11y = 30$

(d) $7x + 5y = 66$
$\quad\ \ x + \ y = 10$

(e) $x - 2y = 27$
$\quad\ x + \ y = 0$

(f) $5x - \ y = 36$
$\quad\ 2x - 3y = 17$

Solutions:

(a) $x = 5, y = 3$ (b) $x = 3, y = 2$ (c) $x = 1, y = 2$
(d) $x = 8, y = 2$ (e) $x = 9, y = -9$ (f) $x = 7, y = -1$

Let us now look at some problems which lead to simultaneous equations.

Example 1

A book retailer stocks two editions of *How to do Mathematical Investigations*, i.e. the paperback and the hardback edition. One year a school ordered 30 copies of the paperback edition and 100 copies in hardback. The cost to the school was £1280. The same year a college requested 50 copies in paperback and 210 in hardback. The college was charged £2610.

Calculate the cost of each edition of the book that year.

Solution:

Let the cost of the paperback edition be £x.
Let the cost of the hardback edition be £y.

From the school's bill we can form the equation $\quad 30x + 100y = 1280$
From the college's bill we can form the equation $\quad 50x + 210y = 2610$

We shall now attempt to solve the equations simultaneously as before.

$30x + 100y = 1280$ —— ①
$50x + 210y = 2610$ —— ②

We shall eliminate the x term by multiplying equation ① by 5 and equation ② by −3 (negative 3).

$150x + 500y = 6400$ —— ①
$-150x - 630y = -7830$ —— ②

Now adding ① and ② together we obtain

$\phantom{\text{i.e.}\quad}-130y = -1430$
i.e. $130y = 1430$
and so $y = 11$

We are now able to find the value of x by substituting 11 for y in the original equation ①, $30x + 100y = 1280$

which now reads as $\quad 30x + 1100 = 1280$
and so $30x = 180$
giving $x = 6$

We can conclude that the cost of the paperback book was £6 and the cost of the hardback book was £11.

Diagram for Example 2 on page 82

Example 2

A Boeing 747 Jumbo Jet flies from Heathrow, London, to Dorval, Montreal, at an average cruising speed of 480 m.p.h.

On the return journey, the plane travels the same distance but is able to cruise at an average speed of 540 m.p.h. with the aid of the 'jet stream', a wind which blows from west to east.

Calculate the speed of the 'jet stream'.

Find the cruising speed of the plane if there had been no 'jet stream' effect.

Solution:

Let the average speed of the plane without 'jet stream' be p m.p.h.
Let the speed of the 'jet stream' be j m.p.h.

From the journey to Montreal we can form the equation
$$p - j = 480 \quad \text{①}$$
From the journey to London we can form the equation
$$p + j = 540 \quad \text{②}$$
Adding ① and ② gives $2p = 1020$
and so $p = 510$

Substituting 510 for p in equation ② gives $510 + j = 540$
and so $j = 30$

Conclusion:

The speed of the 'jet stream' is 30 m.p.h.

The Boeing 747 would cruise at 510 m.p.h. without the 'jet stream' effect.

Exercise

1. The driver of a VW arrives at a petrol station and buys 30 litres of petrol and a litre of oil. He is charged £15.10.

   A Volvo driver then arrives and pays £25.10 for 38 litres of petrol and 5 litres of oil.

   Calculate the cost of petrol per litre and the cost of oil per litre.

2. Jimmy counted 36 chickens and cows in his farm. He counted 100 legs altogether. How many chickens and how many cows were there?

3. For the sequence 4, 10, 16, 22, ..., the nth term takes the form $an + b$ where a and b are numbers.
   (i) Using the first and second terms of the sequence, write down two equations in a and b and hence find the values of a and b.
   (ii) Using your answer to part (i), find the 100th term of the series.

4. For the series $7 + 11 + 15 + 19 + \ldots$, the sum to 1 term is 7, i.e. $S_1 = 7$, the sum to 2 terms is $7 + 11$, i.e. $S_2 = 7 + 11$, the sum to 3 terms is $7 + 11 + 15$, i.e. $S_3 = 7 + 11 + 15$, etc.
   (i) If the sum to n terms, denoted by $S_n = an^2 + bn$, by forming two equations, find the values of a and b.
   (ii) Hence, find the sum of $7 + 11 + 15 + 19 + \ldots$ to 50 terms, i.e. S_{50}.

Solutions:

1. Cost of petrol = 45 pence per litre. Cost of oil = £1.60 per litre.
2. Number of chickens = 22. Number of cows = 14.
3. (i) $a = 6$ and $b = -2$.   (ii) 598.
4. (i) $a = 2$ and $b = 5$.   (ii) 5250.

Solution to Investigation 17:   *Trees*

We may set up equations from the five accounts.

Let the cost of each Scots Pine be £P
Let the cost of each Sitka Spruce be £S

Calculus Castle	: $50P + 40S = 160$	……………①
Erskine Estate	: $100P + 90S = 335$	……………②
Geometric Gardens :	$10P + 80S = 125$	……………③
Haddock House	: $5P + 10S = 25$	……………④
Gorky Park	: $60P + 40S = 180$	……………⑤

If each customer has been charged the same price for the trees then by solving any pair of the above equations we should obtain the same answers for P and S.

Let us start with equations ① and ②
$\qquad 50P + 40S = 160$ …………… ①
$\qquad 100P + 90S = 335$ …………… ②

We shall multiply equation ① by −2
$$-100\,P - 80\,S = -320 \quad\ldots\ldots\ldots\ldots\ ①$$
$$100\,P + 90\,S = 335 \quad\ldots\ldots\ldots\ldots\ ②$$

Adding ① and ② we obtain
$$10\,S = 15$$
and so $\quad S = 1\cdot 5$

Substituting 1·5 in place of S in equation ① gives
$$50\,P + 40\,(1\cdot 5) = 160$$
$$50\,P + 60 \quad\quad\ = 160$$
$$50\,P \quad\quad\quad\quad\ = 100$$
$$P \quad\quad\quad\quad\quad\ = 2$$

and so from equations ① and ② it seems that the trees may be priced at £2 for Scots Pine and £1.50 for Sitka Spruce.

However, perhaps Calculus Castle or Erskine Estate was wrongly priced.

Let us now group another pair of equations together.
$$10\,P + 80\,S = 125 \quad\ldots\ldots\ldots\ldots\ ③$$
$$5\,P + 10\,S = 25 \quad\ldots\ldots\ldots\ldots\ ④$$

We shall multiply equation ④ by −2.
$$10\,P + 80\,S = 125 \quad\ldots\ldots\ldots\ldots\ ③$$
$$-10\,P - 20\,S = -50 \quad\ldots\ldots\ldots\ldots\ ④$$

Adding ③ and ④ gives us
$$60\,S = 75$$
Hence $\quad S = 1\cdot 25$

Substituting 1·25 for S in equation ③ gives
$$10\,P + 80\,(1.25) = 125$$
$$10\,P + 100 \quad\quad\ = 125$$
$$10\,P \quad\quad\quad\quad\ = 25$$
$$P \quad\quad\quad\quad\quad\ = 2\cdot 5$$

The cost of the trees this time appears to be £2.50 per Scots Pine and £1.25 per Sitka Spruce.

Conclusion:

The customers are correct in that there is obviously some anomaly.

Now we must endeavour to find the true cost of the trees and to determine which customer (or customers) was/were charged the wrong price.

We shall test the first results obtained from solving equations ① and ② simultaneously, i.e. £2 per Scots Pine and £1.50 per Sitka Spruce, by substituting these values into equations ③, ④ and ⑤ in order to see if they satisfy the equations.

10 P + 80 S becomes 10 (2) + 80 (1.50) = 20 + 120 = 140 ≠ 125.
The values do not satisfy equation ③.

5 P + 10 S becomes 5 (2) + 10 (1.50) = 10 + 15 = 25.
The values do satisfy equation ④.

60 P + 40 S becomes 60 (2) + 40 (1.50) = 120 + 60 = 180.
The values do satisfy equation ⑤.

Conclusion:

We can now conclude that there was a discrepancy and that either customer Geometric Gardens was undercharged or the other four customers were overcharged.

In answer to the question, "was their claim justified?", the answer is "yes" but their claim resulted in Geometric Gardens being charged £140 instead of £125.

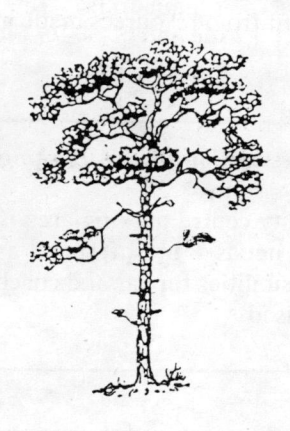

8. How to Find All the Solutions to a Problem

Question

Is it possible to solve **one** equation which contains two distinct variables?

Answer

Strange as it may seem at first, the answer is yes.

Students should attempt to solve the following investigations before reading on to the next section.

Let us consider some very common practical problems which people in managerial positions are frequently faced with — how to take maximum benefit from resources made available to them.

Investigation 18: *A Parking Problem*

A city centre parking area is 1260 m^2. Council regulations state that each car needs 8 m^2 of space and each coach requires 25 m^2. Find **all** the possibilities for car and coach parking in order that the parking area is fully utilised.

Solution on page 88

Investigation 19: *Ensuring a Profit*

City Rail runs an overnight train from Aberdeen to London. Some coaches have 'sleeper' accommodation, whereas others have seats. Passengers travelling in sleepers pay £50 each for the journey and those with seats are charged £40.

For this route to be profitable, City Rail must not let the income for this journey fall below £5000.

Investigate the minimum numbers of each type of passenger CR could take within the specified parameters.

Solution on page 90

Investigation 20: *Town Planning*

A building developer wishes to build two types of houses on a piece of land. Four-bedroomed villas including garden require a minimum area of 700 m² and two-bedroomed bungalows require 300 m². The developer wishes to maximise his profit by ensuring that he uses the whole 12 500 m² area of land.

The developer must submit a number of different plans to the district council planning department for their consideration.

Investigate the proposals which the developer should put forward.

Solution on page 90

Investigation 21: *Penicillin*

It is vital that a doctor administers to a patient the correct dosage of penicillin. She can prescribe tablets each containing 5 units of penicillin or capsules each containing 9 units of penicillin.

The correct dosage is 108 units. Find all the possible combinations of tablets and capsules to ensure that the exact dosage is administered.

Solution on page 91

---

*Euler's Method for finding **all** possible solutions*

Swiss-born Leonhard Euler (pronounced Lenard Oiler), arguably the greatest 18th century mathematician, developed a method for finding all possible solutions to a linear equation involving two variables, x and y say, where both x and y are integers ($\ldots, -3, -2, -1, 0, 1, 2, 3, \ldots$).

His method enables us to find all the possible solutions to many practical problems involving two variables.

Solution to Investigation 18: *A Parking Problem*

Let the number of cars be x.
Let the number of coaches be y (note that x and y must be whole numbers).

As each car requires 8 m² and each coach requires 25 m², we are able to set up an equation

$$8x + 25y = 1260$$

We shall now rewrite this equation making the variable with the smallest coefficient the subject of the mathematical sentence.

$$8x = 1260 - 25y$$

$$x = \frac{1260}{8} - \frac{25}{8}y$$

$$x = 157\tfrac{4}{8} - 3\tfrac{1}{8}y$$

(This may be an unorthodox way of expressing the right-hand side, but it is relevant to the method.)

We shall now split the expression into whole numbers and fractions.

$$x = 157 - 3y + \tfrac{4}{8} - \tfrac{1}{8}y$$

$$x = 157 - 3y + \tfrac{1}{8}(4 - y)$$

We shall now introduce another single variable, α, to take the place of the fractional part of the expression.

and so $\alpha = \tfrac{1}{8}(4 - y)$

giving $8\alpha = 4 - y$
and so $y = 4 - 8\alpha$

Now since y has to be a whole number, it follows that $4 - 8\alpha \geq 0$
Hence $4 \geq 8\alpha$

$$\tfrac{1}{2} \geq \alpha$$

i.e. we now have an upper limit for the value of α.

Again $y = (4 - 8\alpha)$.

We shall now substitute this into the original equation $8x + 25y = 1260$, to give $8x + 25(4 - 8\alpha) = 1260$.

$8x + 100 - 200\alpha = 1260$

$8x = 1160 + 200\alpha$

$x = 145 + 25\alpha$

Again, since x has to be a whole number, it follows that $145 + 25\alpha \geq 0$.

Hence $25\alpha \geq -145$

and so $\alpha \geq -5\frac{4}{5}$.

We now have a lower limit for the value of α.

Therefore $-5\frac{4}{5} \leq \alpha \leq \frac{1}{2}$.

But since x, y and hence α are integers the only values which α could take are $-5, -4, -3, -2, -1$ and 0.

It follows that x (which is equal to $145 + 25\alpha$) could be 20, 45, 70, 95, 120 and 145.

Correspondingly, y (which is equal to $4 - 8\alpha$) could be 44, 36, 28, 20, 12 and 4.

Our conclusion could be presented in a table.

In order to make maximum use of the city centre parking area, any one of the following arrangements could be recommended.

Number of Cars	20	45	70	95	120	145
Number of Coaches	44	36	28	20	12	4

Solution to Investigation 19: *Ensuring a Profit*

$-25 \leq \alpha \leq 0$ and so the possibilities for the least number of each type of passenger to ensure profitability are

Number of Sleeping Passengers	100	96	92	88	84	80
Number of Seated Passengers	0	5	10	15	20	25

Number of Sleeping Passengers	76	72	68	64	60	56
Number of Seated Passengers	30	35	40	45	50	55

Number of Sleeping Passengers	52	48	44	40	36	32
Number of Seated Passengers	60	65	70	75	80	85

Number of Sleeping Passengers	28	24	20	16	12	8
Number of Seated Passengers	90	95	100	105	110	115

Number of Sleeping Passengers	4	0				
Number of Seated Passengers	120	125				

Solution to Investigation 20: *Town Planning*

Let the number of villas be x.
Let the number of bungalows be y.

To use all of the land $700x + 300y = 12\,500$
or $\qquad\qquad\qquad 7x + 3y = 125$

Using the method shown, we obtain $x = 2 - 3\alpha$
and $\qquad\qquad\qquad\qquad\qquad y = 37 + 7\alpha$.

It is found that $-5\frac{2}{7} \leq \alpha \leq \frac{2}{3}$.

But since x, y and hence α must be integers $-5 \leq \alpha \leq 0$.

The table below shows that there are six plans which could be submitted.

Number of Villas	17	14	11	8	5	2
Number of Bungalows	2	9	16	23	30	37

In certain circumstances we may have to introduce a second variable in order to remove all fractions. The following solution shows that, having introduced the parameter α, we then have to make a second substitution.

Solution to Investigation 21: *Penicillin*

Let the number of tablets be x.
Let the number of capsules be y.

For correct dosage $5x + 9y = 108$
and so $5x = 108 - 9y$
hence $x = \dfrac{108}{5} - \dfrac{9}{5}y$
$x = 21\dfrac{3}{5} - 1\dfrac{4}{5}y$
$x = 21 - y + \dfrac{3}{5} - \dfrac{4}{5}y$

Let $\alpha = \dfrac{3}{5} - \dfrac{4}{5}y$
hence $5\alpha = 3 - 4y$
and so $4y = 3 - 5\alpha$
giving $y = \dfrac{3}{4} - 1\dfrac{1}{4}\alpha$ [*] (Note that this time fractions are still prevalent at this stage in the working.)
$y = \dfrac{3}{4} - \alpha - \dfrac{1}{4}\alpha$
$y = -\alpha - \dfrac{1}{4}\alpha + \dfrac{3}{4}$

Now to remove fractions we shall introduce a second variable β.

Let $\beta = -\dfrac{1}{4}\alpha + \dfrac{3}{4}$
and so $4\beta = -\alpha + 3$
giving $\alpha = 3 - 4\beta$ (no fractions)

We may substitute this value for α into equation marked [*] on the previous page, whereupon all fractions will be removed.

$y = \frac{3}{4} - \frac{5}{4}(3 - 4\beta)$

$4y = 3 - 5(3 - 4\beta)$

$4y = 3 - 15 + 20\beta$

$4y = -12 + 20\beta$

$y = -3 + 5\beta$ (note that all fractions have been removed)

Now $y \geqslant 0$ (since we cannot have a negative number of capsules)

and so $-3 + 5\beta \geqslant 0$

$5\beta \geqslant 3$

$\beta \geqslant \frac{3}{5}$ (we now have a lower limit for β)

Our task now is to find an upper limit for β.

Substitute $y = -3 + 5\beta$ into the original equation connecting x and y, $5x + 9y = 108$.

This gives $5x + 9(-3 + 5\beta) = 108$

$5x - 27 + 45\beta = 108$

$5x + 45\beta = 135$

$x + 9\beta = 27$

$x = 27 - 9\beta$

Now $x \geqslant 0$ (since we cannot have a negative number of tablets)

Hence $27 - 9\beta \geqslant 0$

$27 \geqslant 9\beta$

$3 \geqslant \beta$ (we now have an upper limit on β)

Hence $\frac{3}{5} \leqslant \beta \leqslant 3$

as x, y and hence β must be integers, the only suitable values for β are 1, 2 and 3.

Again $x = 27 - 9\beta$ and $y = 5\beta - 3$

Putting β = 1, we have $x = 18$ and $y = 2$
Putting β = 2, we have $x = 9$ and $y = 7$
Putting β = 3, we have $x = 0$ and $y = 12$.

Conclusion:

The correct dosage of penicillin could be administered in three ways

18 tablets and   2 capsules
 9 tablets and   7 capsules
 0 tablets and 12 capsules

9. Pascal's Triangle.

Investigation 22: *'Be Careful!'*

The four circles are shown below. The first has 1 point marked on the circumference, the second circle has 2 points marked, the third has 3 points and the fourth has 4. Every point has been joined to every other point.

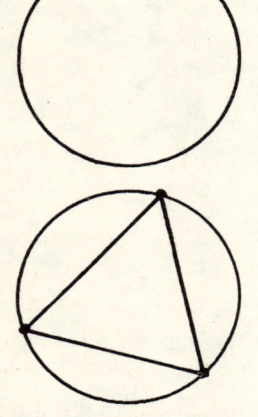

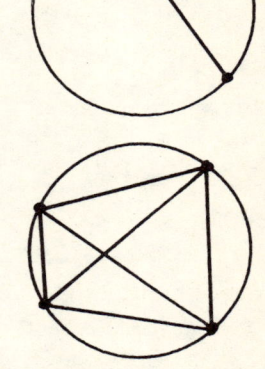

Investigate the relation between the number of points and the number of regions formed as a result of joining the points.

Solutions on page 96

The pattern of numbers below, known as Pascal's Triangle, is named after the celebrated 17th century mathematician, Blaise Pascal.

```
                    1
                  1   1
                1   2   1
              1   3   3   1
            1   4   6   4   1
          1   5  10  10   5   1
        1   6  15  20  15   6   1
```

Complete the next two rows of the triangle. Each number within the triangle is found by adding the pair of numbers above it to its left and right as indicated. Of course the triangle may be continued indefinitely by adding the number 1 to the end of each row.

Pascal's Triangle has many interesting and useful properties in various branches of mathematics but here our aim is to see a connection between the triangle and some investigative problems.

Question 1

One row of numbers is shown in bold type below.

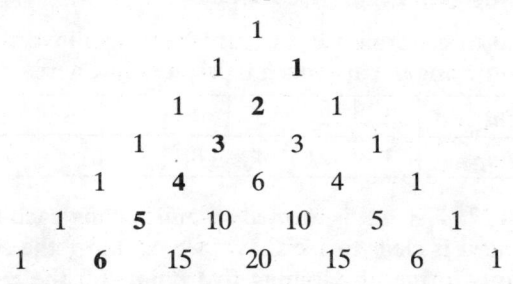

```
                    1
                 1     1
              1     2     1
           1     3     3     1
        1     4     6     4     1
     1     5    10    10     5     1
  1     6    15    20    15     6     1
```

(a) Moving from top to bottom, calculate the sum of the first two numbers in this row.

(b) Moving from top to bottom, calculate the sum of the first three numbers in this row.

(c) Moving from top to bottom, calculate the sum of the first four numbers in this row.

(d) Moving from top to bottom, calculate the sum of the first five numbers in this row.

Note how your answers compare with the row shown in bold type below.

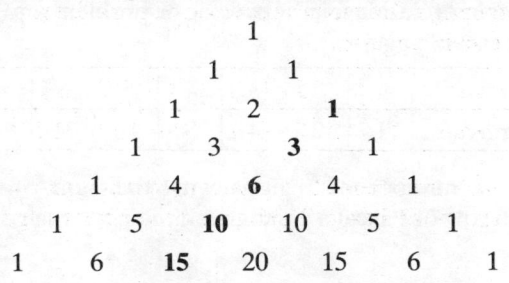

```
                    1
                 1     1
              1     2     **1**
           1     3     3     1
        1     4     **6**     4     1
     1     5    **10**    10     5     1
  1     6    **15**    20    15     6     1
```

Question 2

(a) By multiplying, calculate the values of 11^2, 11^3, 11^4.
(b) Compare your answers to Pascal's Triangle above.
(c) Write down your prediction for the value of 11^5.
(d) Calculate the value of 11^5. *

* This last answer should emphasise to the student that any conjecture must be tested.

Solution to Investigation 22: *'Be Careful!'*

We are expected to generalise in our answer to this investigation. We could attempt to answer using the approach illustrated in Chapter 2.

Number of points	1	2	3	4	5	6	n
Number of regions	1	2	4	8	.	.	.

This sequence, 1, 2, 4, 8, ..., is formed by multiplying each term by 2 to form the next one, and it is clear to see that if we continue the sequence then the number of regions formed by joining five points on the circumference of a circle to each other should be 16 and six points should produce 32 regions.

Check this conjecture by drawing suitable diagrams.

If you have counted the number of regions using 6 points you may have been surprised to find that there are 31 regions and not 32 as you may have anticipated.

Again this result underlines the point of checking conjectures.

Is there no connection between the number of points and the number of regions as described above?

There is an amazing relationship between our problem and Pascal's Triangle. Let us look at our table again.

Number of points	1	2	3	4	5	6	n
Number of regions	1	2	4	8	16	31	

and compare the number of regions with the sum of the boldly typed numbers in each row of Pascal's Triangle on the next page.

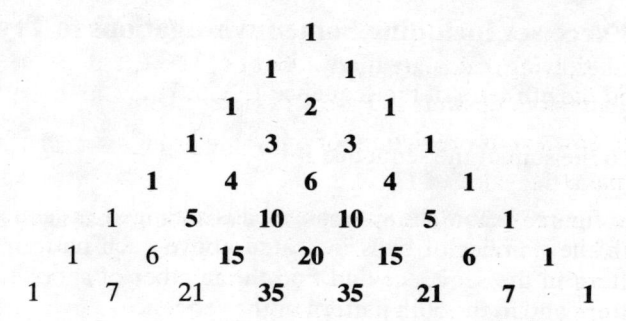

```
                      1
                   1     1
                1     2     1
             1     3     3     1
          1     4     6     4     1
       1     5    10    10     5     1
    1     6    15    20    15     6     1
 1     7    21    35    35    21     7     1
```

The sum of the numbers in bold type in each row is

```
 1
 2
 4
 8
16
31
57
```

The number of regions formed when *n* points on the circumference of a circle are joined is found by taking the sum of the last 5 numbers (if there are 5) in the *n*th row of Pascal's Triangle.

Check by drawing that the number of regions formed when seven points on the circumference of a circle are joined to each other is 57.

Find the number of regions formed when eight points are joined. Use Pascal's Triangle below.

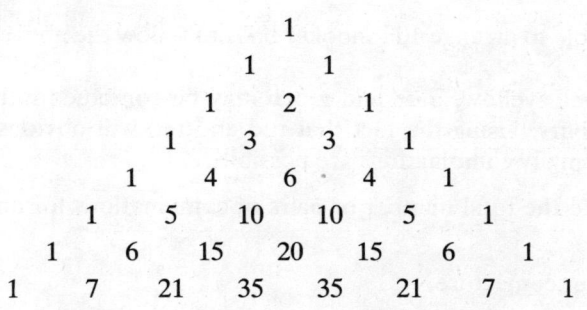

```
                      1
                   1     1
                1     2     1
             1     3     3     1
          1     4     6     4     1
       1     5    10    10     5     1
    1     6    15    20    15     6     1
 1     7    21    35    35    21     7     1
```

Answer: 99

10. Exercises Including Some Investigations to Try Yourself

1. Find the nth term of the sequence $1, 3, 5, 7, \ldots$

2. Find the sum of the sequence $1 + 3 + 5 + 7 + \ldots + n$

3. The figures below show snooker balls arranged in sequences of patterns with the number of balls indicated above each pattern. Draw the next pattern in the sequence and find the number of snooker balls in the nth pattern and in the 50th pattern of the sequence.

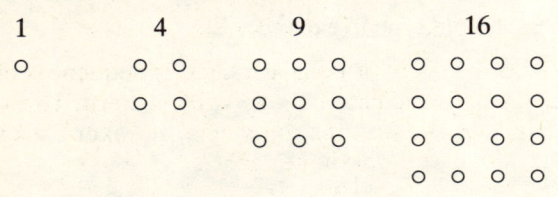

```
   1         4          9            16
   o        o o       o o o        o o o o
            o o       o o o        o o o o
                      o o o        o o o o
                                   o o o o
```

4. The figures below show snooker balls arranged in sequences of patterns with the number of balls indicated above each pattern. Draw the next pattern in the sequence and find the number of snooker balls in the nth pattern and in the 20th pattern of the sequence.

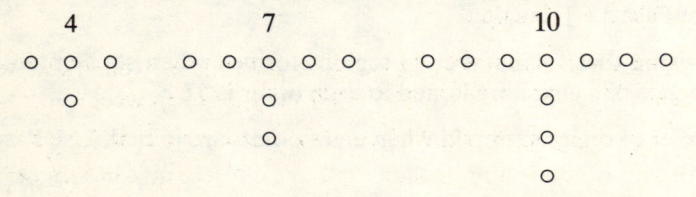

```
    4              7                  10
  o o o        o o o o          o o o o o o
    o              o                  o
                   o                  o
                                      o
```

Is it possible to arrange 100 snooker balls to follow the above pattern?

5. Colours red, yellow, blue and green may be combined in pairs to form other colours. Using the fact that red and red will obviously form red, etc., how many combinations are possible.

Investigate the total number of pairs of combinations for any number of colours.

Check your conjecture.

6. Investigate the total number of triangles pointing upwards enclosed in the figure below. You may wish to consider simpler cases first.

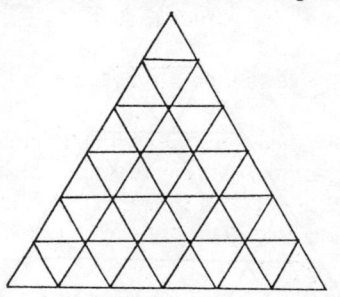

7. The figures below show snooker balls arranged in sequences of patterns with the number of balls indicated above each pattern. Draw the next pattern in the sequence and find the number of snooker balls in the nth pattern and in the 30th pattern of the sequence.

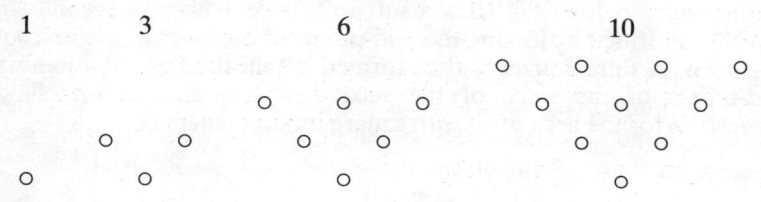

   1   3   6   10

8. Before the summer holidays began, some students remarked to the teacher that they would like a casual job over the seven weeks vacation to earn some pocket money.

   Flippantly, he asked if any of them would be interested in looking after his garden each day for seven weeks.

   He had no takers when he told them the wages: One penny on the first day, two pence on the second day, four pence on the third day, etc.

   Investigate.

9. Investigate how the number of handshakes is related to the number of guests at a party, assuming that each guest shakes hands once with the host and with each of the other guests who has arrived before him.

10. How many regular hexagons are contained in the figure below.

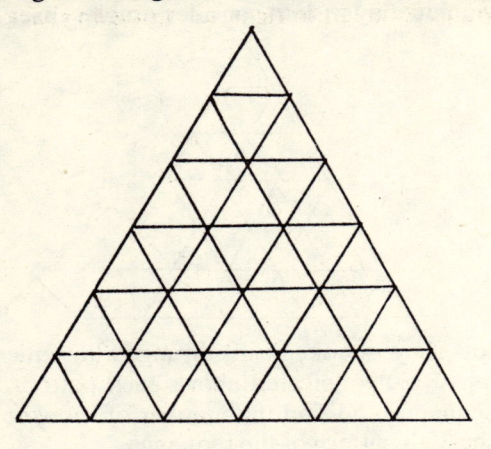

11. In the figure below, PQRS is a square of side 1 unit. A second square VWXY is formed by joining the mid-points of the sides of the first square as shown. A third square is then formed within the figure by joining the mid-points of the sides of the second square and so on. Find an expression for the area of the nth square in the sequence.

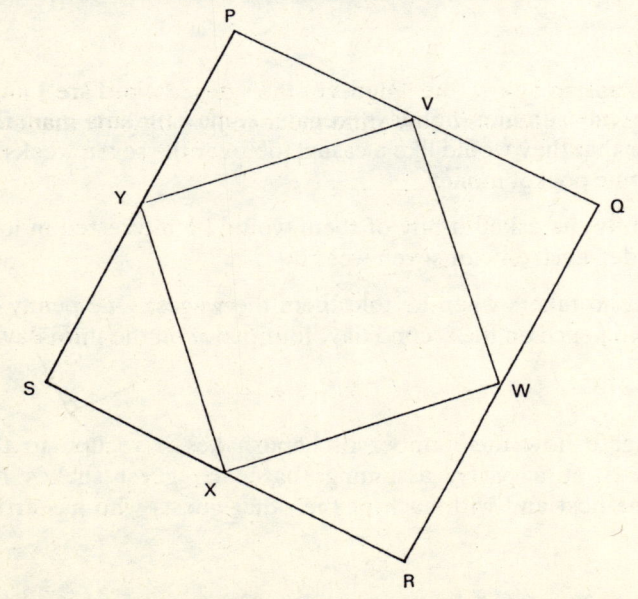

12. Find a formula for the nth term of the sequence 9, 22, 39, 60, 85, . . .

13. How many different paths going from X to Y are in the grid below? Consider only routes from left to right, i.e. not going back.

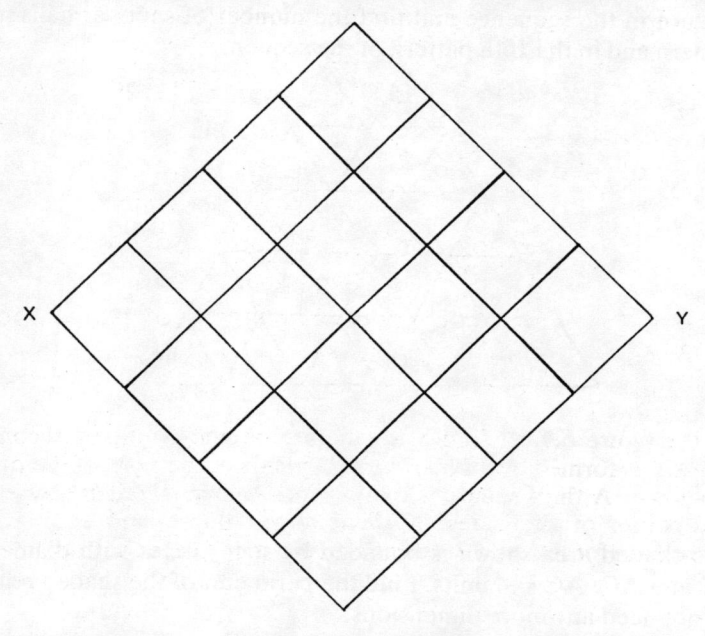

14. In the diagram below, the lengths of the sides marked are 1 unit. Leaving your answer as a square root, find the length of the side marked n.

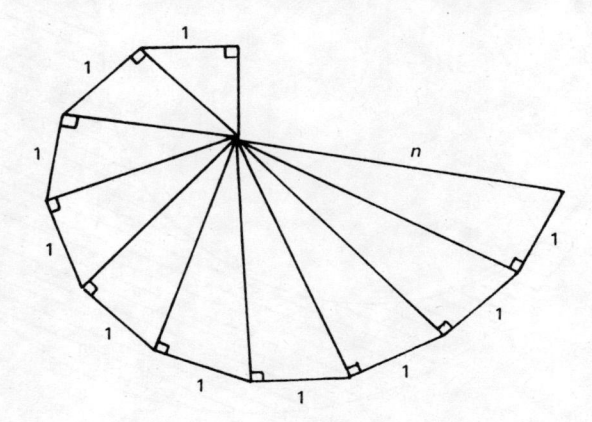

101

15. The figures below show snooker balls arranged in sequences of patterns with the number of balls indicated above each pattern. Draw the next pattern in the sequence and find the number of snooker balls in the nth pattern and in the 10th pattern of the sequence.

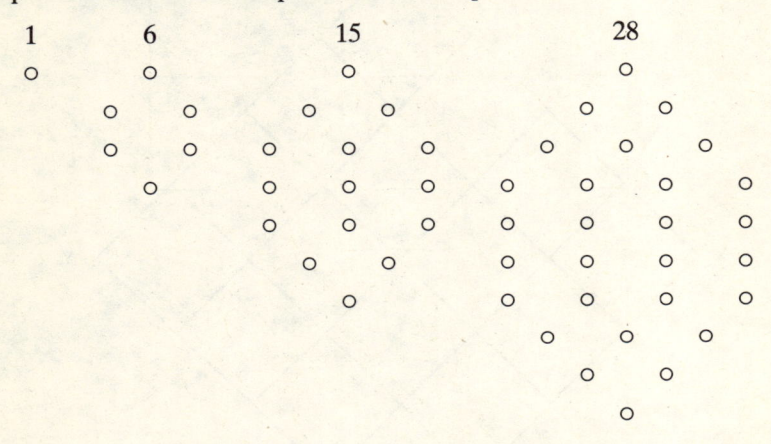

   1   6   15   28

16. The shaded area shown is bounded by semi-circles with diameters AB, BC and AC. AC = 4 units. Find the perimeter of the shaded region. You do not need any more dimensions.

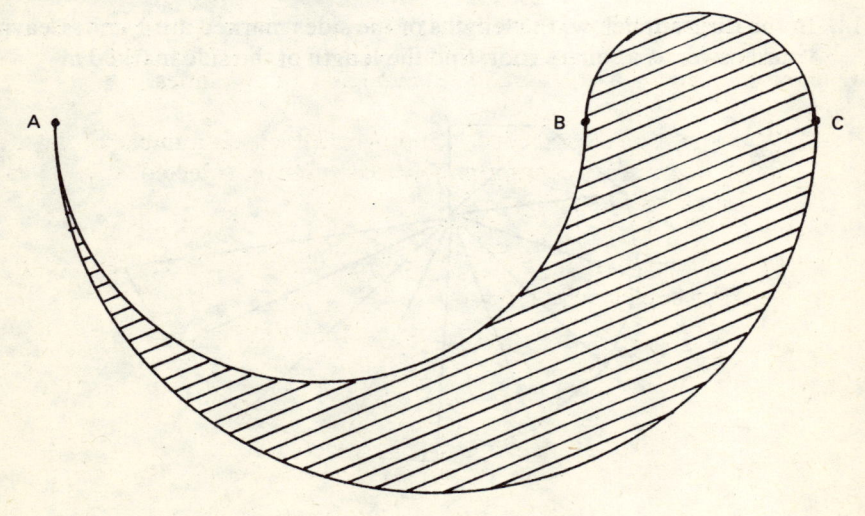

17. A standard set of dominoes contains seven 'doubles'. The 'doubles' from double six to double blank are shown below.

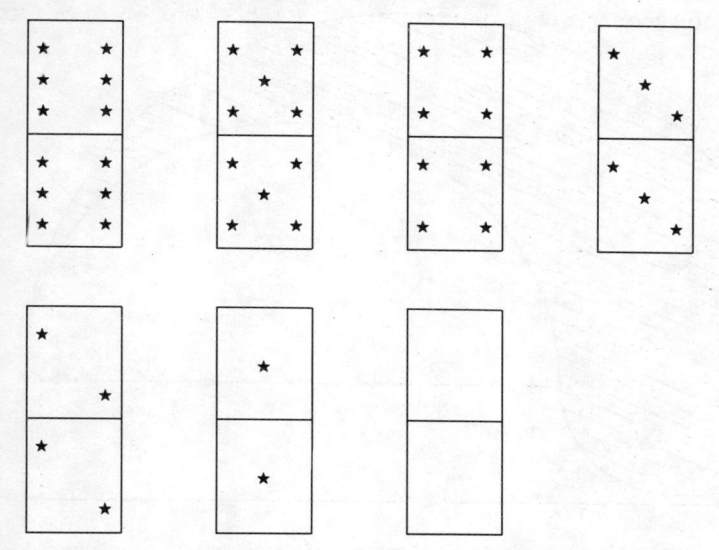

   (a) In your exercise book, or on a separate piece of paper, draw in all the other dominoes, i.e. the 'singles', e.g. six-five, six-four, etc. Remember to work systematically.

   (b) How many dominoes are in a standard set of dominoes?

   (c) With the dominoes placed face down, what total number of spots is most likely to be chosen when a domino is selected at random? Investigate systematically.

   (d) What total number of spots is least likely to be chosen when a domino is selected at random?

18. In the diagram below the shaded area is made up of three semi-circles. Find an expression for its area in terms of x, y and π.

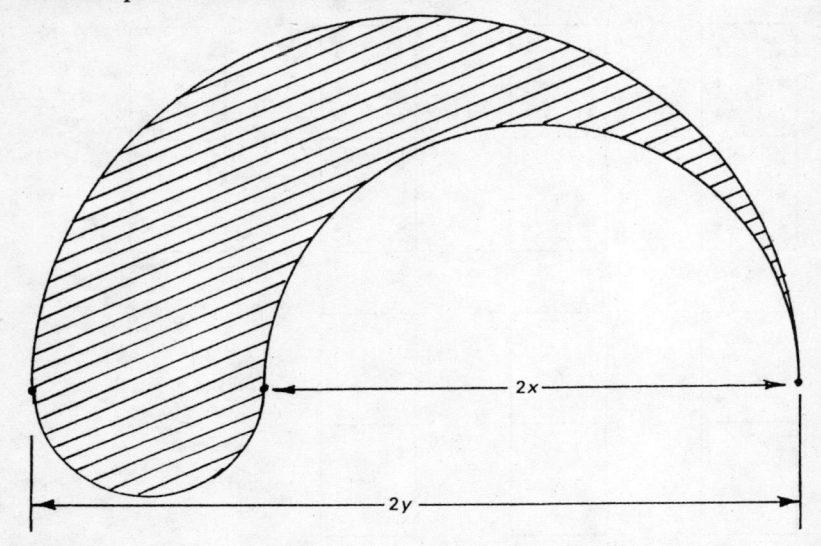

19. The figures below show snooker balls arranged in sequences of patterns with the number of balls indicated above each pattern. Draw the next pattern in the sequence and find the number of snooker balls in the nth pattern and in the 40th pattern of the sequence.

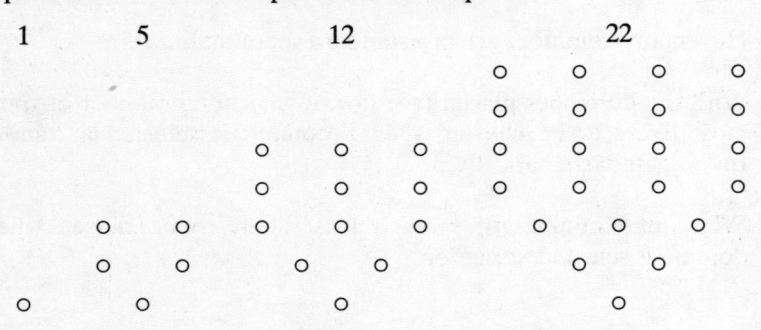

    1   5   12   22

20. A North-East farmer owns some sheep and some ducks. His animals have in total 280 legs and 100 heads. How many sheep and how many ducks does he own?

21. The milkman presented four of his customers with the following bills.

Mrs. MacGregor:
Six cartons of milk plus three cartons of yoghurt £3.24

Dr. MacKay:
Ten cartons of milk plus seven cartons of yoghurt £6.04

Ms MacTavish:
Four cartons of milk plus four cartons of yoghurt £2.40

Oban Arms Hotel:
Twenty cartons of milk plus thirty cartons of yoghurt £17.20

After checking the calculations, one of the customers complained that the bill was incorrect.

Find the cost of the two items and investigate the complaint.

22. Verify that the following statements are true:

$1^3 = 1^2 - 0^2$
$2^3 = 3^2 - 1^2$
$3^3 = 6^2 - 3^2$

Now continue the sequence

$4^3 = 10^2 -$
$5^3 =$
$6^3 =$
.
.
.

Find an expression for n^3 in terms of the above sequence and **hence** evaluate 60^3.

23. British Telecom uses 1 cm diameter cable. The cable of circular cross section is inserted in circular tubes. Investigate the minimum tube diameter required to accommodate four cables as shown below.

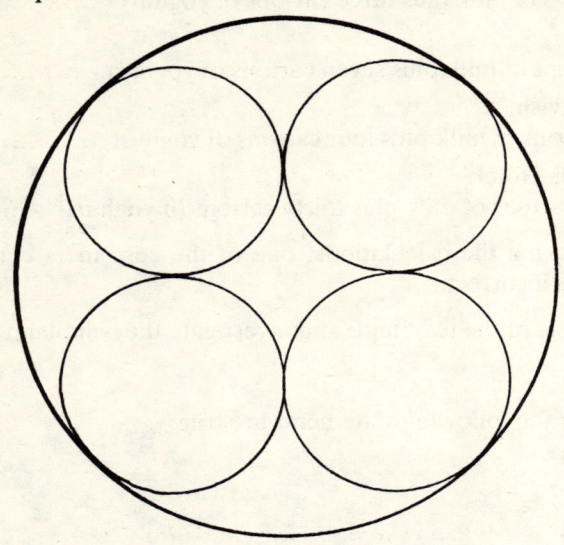

24. Using the information given in problem 23, find the minimum tube diameter necessary to accommodate three BT cables as illustrated below.

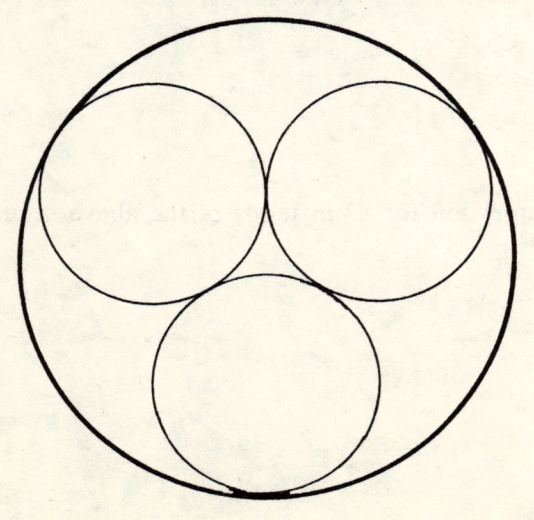

11. Solutions to Exercises

1. nth term $= 2n - 1$

2. Sum to n terms $= n^2$

3. Number in the nth pattern $= n^2$; number in 50th pattern $= 2500$.

4. Number in the nth pattern $= 3n + 1$; number in 20th pattern $= 61$; yes, since the equation $3n + 1 = 100$ produces a value for n which is a whole number.

5. 10; with n colours the number of combinations is $\frac{1}{2}n(n + 1)$.

6. 56.

7. Number in nth pattern is $\frac{1}{2}n(n + 1)$; 465.

8. The wage on the 49th day to 10 significant figures is £2 814 749 767 000. The total wage over the 7-week period is almost double this amount.

9. With n guests, not including the host, there would be $\frac{1}{2}n^2 + \frac{1}{2}n$ handshakes.

10. 18.

11. Area $= \dfrac{1}{2^{n-1}} = 2^{1-n}$ units^2.

12. nth term $= n(2n + 7)$.

13. 20 paths.

14. $\sqrt{11}$

15. Number in the nth pattern $= n(2n - 1)$; 190.

16. 4π units.

17. *b* 28;   (*c*) 6;   *d* 0 or 12.

18. $\pi y(y-x)$.

19. Number in the *n*th pattern is $\frac{1}{2}n(3n-1)$; 2380.

20. Number of sheep = 40; number of ducks = 60.

21. Ms MacTavish was undercharged by 40 pence.

22. $n^3 = \left[\frac{1}{2}n(n+1)\right]^2 - \left[\frac{1}{2}n(n-1)\right]^2$;
    $60^2 = \left[\frac{1}{2}(60)(60+1)\right]^2 - \left[\frac{1}{2}(60)(60-1)\right]^2 = 216\,000$.

23. $\frac{1}{2}(1+\sqrt{2})$ cm.

24. $\left(\frac{1}{2}+\frac{1}{\sqrt{3}}\right)$ cm.

NOTES

NOTES

NOTES

NOTES